Thanks for your
Support!
♡ Maralee

Thanks for your
Support!

— *signature*

Even So

Maralee Mason

WESTBOW
PRESS®
A DIVISION OF THOMAS NELSON
& ZONDERVAN

WestBow Press books may be ordered through booksellers or by contacting:

WestBow Press
A Division of Thomas Nelson & Zondervan
1663 Liberty Drive
Bloomington, IN 47403
www.westbowpress.com
1 (866) 928-1240

Scripture quotations marked (NIV) are taken from the Holy Bible, New
International Version®, NIV®. Copyright © 1973, 1978, 1984, 2011 by Biblica,
Inc.™ Used by permission of Zondervan. All rights reserved worldwide. www.
zondervan.com The "NIV" and "New International Version" are trademarks
registered in the United States Patent and Trademark Office by Biblica, Inc.™

Scripture taken from the New King James Version®. Copyright © 1982
by Thomas Nelson. Used by permission. All rights reserved.

Scripture taken from the King James Version of the Bible.

ISBN: 978-1-9736-8896-9 (sc)
ISBN: 978-1-9736-8897-6 (hc)
ISBN: 978-1-9736-8895-2 (e)

Library of Congress Control Number: 2020905386

Print information available on the last page.

WestBow Press rev. date: 04/21/2020

This book is dedicated
to my Dad and to my brother, Matthew.
'We made it through the fire.'

CONTENTS

Dear Mom,

You were many things, but a mystery was not one of them. It is just one of the things we have in common. My emotions, like yours, are big. There is no hiding them; as hard as I try to, they find their way out. I experience and feel things intensely, and I know you did too. Whatever I experience, I struggle to keep it to myself. There is something deep inside me that is compelled to share my experiences; not just my successes but my failures as well, and I think what compels me is you.

You were often rejected by others because they didn't understand your heart or sensitivity. Even so, where others found weakness, you saw strength. You never stopped feeling and letting yourself be seen, which made you incredibly brave. You inspired me to be brave too, by the way you encouraged me to embrace my emotions and my sensitive heart. You were the most real person I have ever known. Your life was an authentic one. You didn't just share the beauty, you shared the ugliness too. When you were young, you expressed yourself with the hope of being known and loved. As you grew older, you did so with the hope that your story would help someone else. You taught me many things, one of which is that there is not much to learn from a perfect person but there can be much to learn from one's failures and struggles. You were not a mystery and you didn't want to be. Through your life you demonstrated true strength and genuine faith to me and the world, and you constantly showed what courage looked like. You experienced so much, and at times your strength made it hard to see your fear. That's why you were so inspiring. I could see fear in your eyes, but I also saw you face the things that scared you and you did them anyway. I am consumed with my shortcomings, and my past sneaks up on me when I am not looking. I know you doubted yourself; I know you desperately desired to belong; I know you were aware of your faults and wanted to change them, and I know your past often caught you off guard too. I understand your struggles, and if you were here, I know you would understand mine. I take comfort in our similarities even though I know they scared you. You wanted to shield me from the same obstacles you faced; you feared feeling like you doomed me. The thing is, although you were afraid that I would turn out like you, I was so terrified I wouldn't. Because I am like you, I have wrestled many of the same things you did, but because I am like you, I also see things like you. I believe and hope like you. I laugh and sing like you. I give and love like you. I am not a mystery, and because of your example, I don't want to be.

Our relationship is a complex one. You are the one I admire most but also the one who has caused me the most pain. Every single day I wrestle with this. Every day, I struggle with this imbalance—battling between honouring you and forgiving you. I lived a long time only holding one or the other, which I found difficult. I had to constantly choose between acknowledging my feelings or honouring your memory. So I started to make space for both.

But no matter how much harm you and your illness caused, my love for you runs deep and strong. It runs through the anger and through my pain. I get closer to healing when I acknowledge both sides—when I accept the wounds you gave and the hopeful example you laid out before me. At the end of the day, your good outweighs the bad, it just doesn't erase it.

Even as I grapple with the complexity of my feelings, I still look to you when I am at a loss as to how to move forward. Even though you are gone, your voice still guides me. Time has passed, but your footprints have not faded. I walk carefully in them for I know they will lead me somewhere truly breathtaking.

I tell your story because you can no longer tell it. I bare it all as you taught me to. I love others like you did. I believe even when it's not easy, and I let my vulnerability show even though I'm scared to. I was so destroyed when you died. I felt broken because you took a piece of me with you, now I take comfort in that. I am at peace knowing that a piece of me lives with you.

I feel your absence every day. I hear you when I sing and see you when my children smile. I'll miss you always. I'll love you forever.

Forever your daughter,
Maralee

Walking Through Fire

"I hate my life," is something I often mumbled under my breath. I said this phrase more times throughout my life than I would care to admit. My life felt so hard, too hard. "Shouldn't life be better than this?" It was a question I wrestled with daily. That question was almost my demise because I was never content with my circumstance; I wanted easier, I wanted better, which kept me unsatisfied and bitter.

As a little girl, I had no idea where life was going to take me, what I was going to do, or who I was going to become. I had witnessed many things during that time—I saw suffering, great sorrow, and loss. As I watched these things happen around me, as I grew and life started to get more difficult, questions about the nature of my own character entered my mind. I would ask myself, "How will I handle tragedy? What will I do if things do not get better, but get worse? Could I cope with unbelievable heartbreak? Am I strong enough to endure what life may throw my way?"

These questions were always looming in my mind. I often dismissed them, maybe out of innocence, maybe out of arrogance, but most likely because I was afraid of the answers. I could wonder all day long. I could imagine that when times got bad, I would be strong and brave. It wasn't until I felt the kind of pain that crippled me from deep within my soul, until I cried tears of loss that never seemed to stop flowing, that I knew how I would deal with tragedy. I couldn't know until I was in the midst of it. And as I stood surrounded in loss, I was disappointed because I was not as brave or as strong as I had hoped I would be.

It was easy to say I could conquer anything when I was on the outside looking in, but it was a different story when I was thrown into the center of a raging fire, a fire so strong it seemed to never stop burning, a fire that fed off everything around me, a fire that kept getting bigger until it swallowed me whole. But in the fire is where I realized that I was no better or stronger than anyone else.

It wasn't until my family was facing the unthinkable that we discovered who we really were and what we were made of. It took being smacked in the face with life's harsh winds to bring just enough tears to our eyes to cause us to see things differently. Once you are in the middle of hardship and your attitudes are put to the test, you will discover how very difficult and painful the trials of life can be.

I once watched a glassblower at work. The artist would make an incredible creation by rolling a metal rod through some molten glass and putting it into the hot fire. The raging fire melted the glass so it could be shaped. And at the end of the glassblower's work, something beautiful emerged. As a family, we were thrown into the fire. It hurt more than words can say; but in the fire we were shaped, made stronger, and at the end, something strong and beautiful was created.

Over time, through many tough lessons, I have learned I cannot predict the future. All I can do is live one day at a time, pray I find strength when I need it, and let the pain I will face in this life shape me and make me new. It took some time, but I have finally realized I do not need to be strong every second of every day. I am not weak because I feel pain and endure struggle. We all struggle. We all need help. For so long, I was ashamed of my struggles and my pain. I felt judged by so many for years, so after a while, I learned to hide my pain and fear. I learned to lean only on myself and carry my burdens on my own. Acting this way went against who I was as a person. I was normally open and honest, but that proved to give me more hurt than I could bear. When I would move somewhere different, I wouldn't tell anyone my past or what my family and I had been through, but living that way almost broke me. I needed to be set free, I needed to let go not just for me but for my children. So I started to write. I poured my soul out onto the paper. I broke outside of what was comfortable. I let what I was holding back come pouring out. And after years of writing, I decided to truly let go and no longer be ashamed of where I have been or who I used to be. In this book, I share it all. I hold nothing back. Nothing is really told in order. I group the positives together and the negatives together. But in reality, it was all intertwined. The good and the bad were woven together. I want to share my past and the story of my mother and her faith. I want to share the lessons I have learned and the ones my mother has taught me. I want to share all of my struggles and fears I have faced and continue to face in the hopes that it gives comfort, encouragement, and hope.

CHAPTER ONE

Kathleen

"For I know the plans I have for you," declares the LORD,
"Plans to prosper you and not to harm you,
plans to give you hope and a future."
Jeremiah 29:11, NIV

I was crying so hard I was almost screaming. I was running as fast as my little legs could go. My eyes were fixed on my destination. I didn't look back, not oven once. I barreled down the street where I lived feeling like I would never make it home. When I turned onto my driveway, I felt such relief. I bolted up the incline, running out of breath with my eyes glued to my front door, just longing to be home. I scared my mother when I burst through our front door, slamming it behind me. When she got to our entryway to see who was there, she found me face first on the steps, weeping.

"What are you doing home? Why are you not in school?" she asked.

I was crying so hard I couldn't answer why I had left my kindergarten class in the middle of the day. She quickly called my school to let them know where I was. As she talked to my school, I sat there terrified that she would make me go back. My mother hung up the phone and sat me up on the step, looked into my eyes,

1

and brushed my hair out of my face. She didn't seem mad at all, just concerned. She took my hand and led me to my room and sat me down on my bed and sat down next to me. She wrapped her arm around my shoulders. She just held me for a while before asking me what was going on. I began to tell her about the older boy at school who had been bullying me and how it happened again that day. Through my sobbing, I told her how he would call me terrible names and throw things at me. How he would yell awful words at me while hanging out of the school bus window as I walked home from school. I confessed to my mom how scared of him I was and how much he was hurting my feelings. That day when that boy teased me for the hundredth time, something happened in my heart. It was like my soul could not take any more. My instincts kicked in. I had to protect myself somehow, so I bolted. I ran away. I ran to the safest place I knew.

My mom listened to my every word intently, secretly struggling as it broke her heart to see her baby hurting. When my crying slowed, my mother took her hand and slowly started rubbing my back in a circular motion. As she did, she said to me softly, "Everything will be all right. His mean words don't matter. It doesn't change who you are. Let his and all other unkind words flow off you like water off a duck's back."

Her words and just her hand on my back gave such comfort to my little wounded heart. My mother knew more than anyone what it was like to be hurt by others. What it was like to be knocked down by others' words. She knew what to say to me that day because she knew how I felt. She had been in that place before. She had been rejected and left behind. She had faced enough disappointment to last a lifetime. So, when she looked into my teary eyes that day, she saw herself. After that day, she kept seeing more of herself in me. She noticed I had a passion similar to hers, a sensitive soul, a heart and boldness like hers, a struggle to control my tongue like she had. Although she loved how similar we were, it also terrified her. Those things we had in common were the things that often led her to a broken heart. So, every day she prayed for me with a passion that never dimmed and with fear in her heart because she did not want me to ever have to face the same hard things she did.

Kathleen Margaret Turner was born on October 9, 1955. From an early age, I knew my mom's childhood was complicated and intense. I don't know exactly what happened in her house growing up since I wasn't there and it's incredibly difficult to write about something I wasn't around for. But I know I can't leave this part out; it is vital to show where my mother started so you can see how fabulously she finished. So, I will not speak for anyone else. Instead I will share with you what I know for sure—what was told to me and what I understand.

My mom was always honest and open. She hid very little from her children. Although I don't remember her actually telling us, her past and her mistakes were always known to me. There were times I would overhear her talking to my father about her childhood, about how her father treated her. It was evident there was trauma and that what occurred within her childhood affected how she viewed herself. I knew there was violence toward her from childhood up into her second marriage. She struggled daily and had nightmares about the things her father would say to her. She spent so much time wishing she could unhear all the yelling and the threats made against her.

I heard stories of his booming voice that carried throughout the house. I would often find her crying about it, often on my dad's shoulder. I was aware that her dad left the family and worked away and his absence came as a relief. Her parents' problems seemed to swallow the family whole. The way her parents lived their lives was the only example she had to follow, which would lead her down paths that usually ended in tears, emptiness, and an aching in her heart she learned to ignore. As she grew up, she wished she could be anywhere but home. It was too difficult to watch her parents spiraling downward and deal with the pain that came with it. But at the end of the day, it did not matter what they did or didn't do

— they were still her parents and she never for a second stopped loving them, which made everything that much harder.

My grandparents divorced while my mother still lived at home. I never knew my mom's parents as a couple; I only knew them with their new spouses — people I loved dearly. I always felt blessed having two sets of grandparents on one side of the family. My Papa, my mom's dad, lived close to us, fifteen minutes away to be precise. She must have reached some sort of place of forgiveness with her dad as we saw him often, which couldn't have been done if she hadn't forgiven him. I think about how hard that must have been for her sometimes. I think of how he probably reminded her of all the pain she had to endure. But her desire for us to have her parents, especially her dad, in our lives was important to her; she wanted us to have a grandpa. I do not think the process was immediate or easy. It was constant, ongoing, a daily decision to forgive him for the past in order to have a future with him in it.

I remember my Papa and his wife being at every one of my birthdays, bringing along a crisp ten-dollar bill placed inside a beautiful card. We spent most Christmas dinners at their house. I remember how much I loved the way they decorated their Christmas tree. It didn't feel like Christmas to me if they were not there.

But on the other side of things, I also recall his breath often smelling of alcohol, although I didn't know what that smell was until I was a teenager. I remember during most of our visits, he would get very angry about something and would raise his voice. He could be scary but also gentle and kind. I remember him teaching me how to drive and him being terrified as I tried to navigate the road. He would pick me and Matthew up most afternoons from school, which we always looked forward to. He was always a big part of my life. And I liked having him in it. After James and I got engaged, he took the time to give me and James dancing lessons so we could wow our guests during our first dance. I remember him being frustrated and baffled that I didn't share his good dancer genes and truly amazed at how bad we were, but it made for lots of laughter and one of my favorite memories.

When it came to my grandma, I never heard my mom talk negatively about her. But I had the sense there was some issues there. My grandma was kind and sweet. I loved her company. She didn't always live close, but we saw her and her husband often and I always looked forward to our visits.

My grandparents worked hard at changing themselves. They left their past behind them and became wonderful people — the parents their kids deserved and the most caring and loving grandparents. Though the hurt they caused during my mother's childhood could never be erased, my grandparents tried to right all their wrongs, showing love to my mom and her children as often as they could. Even though my mom deeply appreciated their efforts, which brought them closer, she was still haunted and wounded so deeply she thought at times she would never recover. But at the end of all the hurt and pain, her parents ended up being a great example to her. They taught her that no matter what you have done in the past or who you used to be, there is hope. You can change and you can find what you are looking for.

When my grandma was in the hospital dying, my papa went to see her. He was there visiting my mom who was in a room down the hall. He started walking down the hall toward his ex-wife's room, his hands visibly shaking. He stopped just short of the door, turned around to me, and said, "What am I going to say to her? What should I say?"

I was just eighteen and not quite sure what he should say. I hugged my papa and said, "Just tell her how you feel. Thank her for what she has given you."

He took a deep breath, nodded his head, and walked into her room. She looked up at him and smiled. He approached her bedside and took her hand tightly in his. He looked in her eyes with tears in his and said, "Thank you for our beautiful children."

The family was gathered around her hospital room door. We

started crying. Some of the family I hadn't seen together in many years. Some, I had never seen together. That moment may not have changed the past, but it helped things move forward.

My mother's teen years were only the beginning of the difficult times she would have to face. The wounds were going to get deeper, the pain more severe, and she was in no way equipped to handle any of it.

My mother had hoped that as her life continued, things would start to look up, but unfortunately, it took many years for her life to change. In my mom's late teen years, she made choices that often put her in danger. She attended parties where she would drink too much and go off with boys she did not know. In many regards, she was like most teenage girls, wanting to have fun, wanting to feel important, and searching for love, usually in the worst possible places. In high school, my mom was quite popular; she had many friends and was well liked. She was free-spirited and had a vibrant personality, so when she joined the cheerleading squad, no one found that odd at all; it was the perfect fit for her. My mom enjoyed high school for the most part; she loved being around people. She loved to talk and laugh with her friends. She loved cheerleading and singing. But at some point, she felt done with it all. I don't know exactly what made her quit; she just seemed to have had enough. After tenth grade, she left school for good.

I think deep down she was bored with her life, filled with a longing for more, and she could not find it where she was.

Her desire for more than what she had, her desire to be still and not have to fight so hard for what she wanted or needed, was so great and her even bigger desire to be loved was so strong, she searched everywhere for it — in every friend she met, in every guy she encountered, in every conversation with her parents. She looked at every party she went to and every band practice she attended. Her mind never stopped thinking about what she never had and her heart never stopped searching for it. She had a void and was willing to do anything to fill it. Men would often take advantage of her drunken state. She would spend her evenings hiding from her life and every morning when she woke up, it was always there waiting for her, often accompanied with shame, confusion, and pain. But my mom kept on searching. She searched in the darkest and loneliest places, in men who did not have love on their minds, in places where love just cannot be found. No matter how unsavory the situations were, she kept going back. Her journey to find what she deeply and secretly longed for cost her more than she ever found. She would open the door to people who were no good, people who did not deserve her trust. The emotional beating she endured from men and friends accentuated her pain. Her brother would often come home to find her crying on the couch in the living room. She was a private person when it came to her life, but it was obvious how let down and broken she was. My mother was filled with anger and hurt — her past and even her present started to take away her hope. Bitterness was starting to take root deep within her soul. She tried not to dwell on it or give it any thought, but as she ignored it, it grew. There was no escaping her past. At seventeen, my mom left home and the town she despised. She moved in with her grandmother whom she loved. She needed a fresh start and decided that was the place to get it. She may not have gotten far, but for her it was just far enough.

Not too long after moving away, she met a man. This man was far from boring. He liked her—more than that, he loved her in his own way. With him, she was not alone. She had someone by her side, or at least the illusion of that. When she saw her new boyfriend, she saw hope. Hope that she was finding what she had always wanted, hope that the void she had been carrying would be filled. For the first time in her life, she fell in love, she thought she found her missing piece. So, she gave everything she had to her man, hoping that love could cover all her pain and injuries, hoping that this love would be enough. She thought that maybe, just maybe, he could be her answer. Because she gave so much of herself to another person, she was left with very little, and because of that, she would end up losing herself.

At eighteen, my mother was taken by complete surprise when she found out she was pregnant. She was in utter shock. She was scared, but deep down it made her happy. She had always wanted a family of her own. This may not have been the kind of excitement my mother had been looking for, but regardless, she was overjoyed. She knew she was meant to be a mother; she just never thought it would happen at such a young age. Shortly after she found out about the pregnancy, she made the decision to marry the father of her baby, partly because she, on some level, really did love him and partly because it seemed like the best decision for her baby. She wanted to give her baby the best life she could. When she gave birth to her son, she instantly fell in love with him. She looked down at Brian and saw perfection, and she vowed to love and protect him always.

Two or so years passed, and my mom slowly started to drift away from her husband. She started to realize that the man she married wasn't close to who she was looking for and that the void she had was somehow growing bigger. Her life was filled with loneliness. My mom made a lot of mistakes in that relationship, one of which being that she did not stick up for herself or for her son. In the midst of her marriage she ended up becoming a woman she despised.

But through all the pain, there was one constant in her life—and that was her son, Brian. When she looked at him, she could see the life they were meant to live, and that gave her hope. She loved him so much, a feeling so intense and powerful she never knew it was possible. He was the one good thing in her life. He was her hope and her light. And because of her deep love for her son, she left her husband and the life that was leading nowhere. She started fresh as a single mother in search of something more, something better for her and for her son. She never really saw that man again. When she left her husband, she had doubts. "A boy needs his father," she would argue to herself, but over time it became evident that her decision was the right one.

Soon after separating from her husband, my mom discovered a shocking and most devastating surprise — she was pregnant for the second time. It was news that should have made her happy. The birth of a baby is supposed to be a blessing. But to my mother, it seemed to be a curse. She was terrified. It all seemed too much for her to handle. She was now carrying the baby of a man she no longer loved, a man who had broken her heart. She had just walked away from him and had no intention of going back, so if she were to have the baby, she would have to do it alone. The thought of raising one child alone scared her; she could not imagine raising two all by herself. And because of that, she made a decision that she would forever regret. She had an abortion. Her doctor told her that it would probably be the best option for her in her situation. She did not know what to do — she assumed the doctor knew best. She had no one to seek advice from; she was alone. Her doctor's advice was all she had, and he was the only one she could turn to. She was so naïve about what an abortion entailed. She went into one of the biggest decisions of her life lightly, and because of that, it almost destroyed her. She had no idea how much that decision would affect her, how much guilt would consume her because of it. She thought she was doing the right thing, but with every passing day, she missed and loved the baby she never knew. It was a regret she wished with all her heart she didn't have. But no matter how hard she wished and hoped, it could not be undone.

My mom was now on her own. The loneliness overwhelmed her, and the pressure was heavily weighing her down. She had to provide for her son without help from anyone. She had to deal with the unbelievable pain and terrible regret from her abortion, and she had to do all of this by herself. At this time in her life, she did not believe in a higher power; she did not rely on any strength but her own, which often seemed to be lacking. Things were dark for my mom. Brian was the only reason she had to keep on going. As she walked the narrow road before her, she hoped to find another reason for breathing. She hoped to find something greater and something better than what she had.

Letters from the Past

My mother was always a bold woman. When she found her life of faith, her boldness intensified. Her faith was of an intense nature—often scaring people away. She spoke often and firmly about Jesus and how much she loved and trusted Him. She also spoke of the devil and how much he had destroyed her. She prayed and spoke to them like they were in the room with her. She believed her words had power and she showed that in the way she prayed. She would tell Jesus of what was in the depths of her heart, and she would ask for forgiveness for her mistakes. She constantly welcomed peace and love into her heart and soul. She would cast out the devil and any negativity in her life; she made it clear that he along with all he'd bring was not welcome.

My mother had lived so long without comfort, without purpose, without direction. It makes sense to me that when she found all of those things and much more that she would pursue it with all she had. People often could not understand or relate to her passion and even I can't fully comprehend it. But I admire it with my whole being. I can hear the beauty in her words, in her desire to be a better person. I hear the beauty in her cries for help, for love, and for forgiveness, beauty in her desire to deny the darkness and her refusal to be ruled by it. My mother and I may have approached faith differently; she may have chosen different words than I would have chosen myself, but I can still see and hear myself in her words. When you listen closely, her words are pretty universal. People were so put off by my mother's intensity that they could not hear the truth in her words, which was a shame because the truth she discovered was a beautiful thing.

(The following are journal entries from after
my mother became a Christian)

March 1985

I pray the Lord will keep me through this. The Lord has shown me today that even when I fall down, I won't fall all the way, for He holds me up with His hand. I have tended to stray from the Presence of God and from his Word lately. I may not be with him, but He is with me.

God does not require anything of me except my confession of sin; this is all He requires of me.

"A broken and a contrite heart [O God,] Thou wilt not despise." [Psalm 51:17, KJV]

We all must try to be honest about our sins to ourselves and to God. We should feel guilty about our sins or else how are we to know that we have done wrong. All we need to do is confess them to Him and our guilt will be gone.

May 1985

I sure am getting sick of the way I am feeling. I went to a Bible study that was on self-esteem.

Wow, do I have a bleak picture of how I see myself. The lady shared on how you can tell if you have low self-esteem: be unorganized, gossiping about other people, always afraid to try anything new, absolutely crumbling under any difficult trial. I have been struggling with this for a year and a half now, and I am really sick of it! Satan is trying to make me take my eyes off Jesus and onto myself, especially my failures. Lord, help me to be wise to Satan and his tricks. Jesus showed me in His Word the other day, in Luke 22:31-32 "Simon, Simon, Satan has asked to sift all of you as wheat. But I have prayed for you, Simon that your faith may not fail. And when you have turned back, strengthen your brothers."

I'm also very sick of the way that I'm acting. Getting mad at Chris [her second husband] for his driving, getting depressed because I can't find anything to wear. Thank You Jesus for giving me a heart of repentance. He has shown me that the struggles I have had in the past couple of years are because there is something inside of me trying to get out!! Jesus is trying to manifest His Spirit in me! Praise His Holy Name!

October 24, 1985
I think God is saying today that He wants me to be self-controlled in all areas of my life (physical, emotional, and spiritual) so that I can be a prayer warrior.

Dear Jesus, I need help to be self-controlled. I also need to be in control of my emotions, i.e., … getting upset with Chris and the kids.

I'm a little like Timothy, fearful and timid. The breakdown of my home as a child affected my ability in later life to develop a proper self-image. That is how Paul encourages us with these words. God has not given us a spirit of fear, but of power and love and a sound mind. God has shown me through His word that he is my all in all. He was with God in the beginning. He still is ruling and reigning today despite all the turmoil there is in the world today. It is safest to trust in a God who raises the dead.

September 1986
I feel the Lord speaking to me today about recognizing sin in my life. Coveting things I see in the store.

Getting frustrated and not turning to Jesus right away. Instead I take it out on the kids or Chris.

Hounding Chris about his actions, expecting immediate results. Lord help in all these things; help me to make a change.

I feel God's gentle nudge today as I lost my temper with Brian… again. Whether I was right or wrong does not matter. What matters is how I react. Confirmed through the Daily Bread:

The darkness of a spirit grown mean and small, fruit shriveled on the vine, bitter to the taste of my companions, burdened to be borne by the brave few who love me still.

No, Lord let the fruit grow lush and sweet a joy to all who taste; the Spirit is a sign of God at work—stronger, fuller, brighter at the end. Lord, let me get home before dark. With each added year, we should become kinder, more gracious, less irritable, and less grumpy.

"But the fruit of the Spirit is love, joy, peace, forbearance, kindness, goodness, faithfulness, gentleness, and self-control. Against such things there is no law." Galatians 5:22-23 NIV

"Search me, God, and know my heart; test me and know my anxious thoughts.

See if there is any offensive way in me and lead me in the way everlasting." Psalm 139:23-24 NIV

This Psalm is everything I want to say to God.

December 1985
God did a marvelous work in me through Chris on Sunday.

Saturday, I started having these terrible remembrances of what I did after I had the abortion.

(Dumping Brian off at my aunt's and spending a week with my brother)

I realize now I felt like an unfit mother and that I was actually going through the grieving process of losing a child. Chris and I were praying together on Sunday night, and I started thinking of what had been on my mind the night before and how it really bothered me. Then Chris started to pray about the abortion I had, which was the gift of knowledge given by the Lord for me. He really ministered to me, and I received an inner healing I didn't really know was bothering me, but God sure did, and He knew that I needed His healing touch—thank You, Jesus!

January 1996

Jesus did a work in my heart on Sunday. I came to church weighed down with a heart that cannot love unconditionally. I went up for prayer, intending to ask for a heart of love from the Father. What happened was that pastor prayed over me with a gift of knowledge about my dad, who would one day come ask for forgiveness! The Holy Spirit hit me with Healing as soon as pastor said this. And whose arms did I find comfort? None other than one of the very ones I had trouble loving! Praise His Name!

The upbringing with my dad has rendered my heart somewhat hard to show love. God showed me that my circumstances in growing up are not my fault, that he is using these very seemingly painful experiences to really show me how to love, for real! I don't have to conjure up love in myself. He is healing my heart and chipping away the stone that envelops my heart, a heart not filled with love put there by me, but love that He has put there—born unto Him!

February 20, 1992

I stopped doing what God had been wanting me to do all along—write down my thoughts and especially my prayers. I've allowed the enemy to rob me—again! But no more with the help of the Holy Spirit. I thank You, Lord, because you have always been there for me. I thank You for Your *mercy and great patience that you have toward me. Even though I have strayed, I sense that You understand why, even though I do not. Yes my feelings of guilt and shame being weak and carnal minded. Even though I feel like I have never been so far away from You, You are still working things out for good, and You will make me triumph like never before. I know that You are dealing with my childhood, and I sense with my dad also. I know I have to face the truth about my past, and it says in Your word that "the truth will set you free." Lord, if it hurts, help me to endure it and not lose heart or faint, but help me to face up to it! I confess to You all my sins; they are so many, please Lord, make me clean and use me.*

February 21, 1992
"Having therefore these promises, dearly beloved, let us cleanse ourselves from all filthiness of the flesh and spirit, perfecting holiness in the fear of God..." 2 Corinthians 7:1 NKJV

Thank You, Jesus for Your word. I have been defiled as a child. my emotions have been damaged. Thank You that You have come to "heal the broken-hearted." My childhood does seem fragmented; some things I do remember, but other things I do not—because I did not feel loved, I was not happy. I felt rejected. Help me to get in touch with my past, heal my emotion; deal with sin in my life. The anger I feel, the disappointment that I can better relate to my family. There is a lot I do not know yet, but I trust You, Lord, to bring me through.

I love You, Jesus,
Amen
Jesus,

Help me forgive myself. I think when I get so down on myself, it's hard for me to continue in fellowship with You because I don't think I am good enough. But Your Word tells me that I am good enough by the blood of Jesus. Thank You, dear Lord, for Your free gift of salvation.

May 20, 1992

Dear Jesus, I find it hard to come to You — I really blew it today losing my cool with Chris and Brian because I thought Chris handled confronting Brian all wrong. I said things to Chris that I never should have said. I called him stupid. God forgive me—I have no right to call anyone stupid. I was called stupid all my life, and here I turn around and say it to the one I love—how I could be so "stupid." Chris isn't the stupid one; I am. I know that the way I treat people and the way I "lose it" is because of the way I was treated in the past, but still, that is no excuse. I blame myself because I should know better. Father help me to see and recognize Satan when he tries to cause division amongst my family. Help Chris and me to stay in prayer and in fellowship with You. Help me not to feel so overwhelmed. Remind me that I can hold myself together, even in a crisis. Grant me wisdom; give me self-control. I refuse any demonic spirit put upon me by my parents. I refuse to let that attach itself to me any longer, be gone from me, in Jesus' name, Amen. Thank You, Jesus, that Satan is bound from me and thank You for forgiving me. Amen

CHAPTER TWO

Finding Grace

Grace means all of your mistakes
now serve a purpose instead of serving shame.
~ Brené Brown

My mother's life was not turning out like she thought it would. Every day she was losing hope and was close to giving up. At the time, my mom did not even believe that God existed, but it would seem He sent someone into her life that would change how she viewed everything. The night that impacted my mom's life forever was just an ordinary one. To her, this night wasn't a particularly important one, just a friend's birthday party. Little did she know she would meet the man that would one day change her life.

Chris spotted her instantly from across the room. He couldn't take his eyes off her. She was the most beautiful woman he had ever seen. He quickly tried to think of the perfect line to sweep her off her feet. After much deliberation, he came up with what he thought to be the perfect plan. He gathered all his courage, and with shaking hands and sweat dripping from his brow, he limped up to her pretending to have injured his foot and asked, "Could I put my feet on your lap?" Although the story of a sore and injured foot was completely made up, my mother, who was trying to be polite, answered, "Yes."

After holding my father's foot for what seemed to be a lifetime, she walked away and kept her distance for the rest of the night. My dad felt defeated; he was in a bad place; he was feeling lower than low. His wife had left him, he recently lost his job, and now he just faced another rejection. He sat at the party quietly watching her have a great time, talking with everyone. Sitting there, he felt so angry at himself for how much he messed things up, not just that night, but every night leading up to it. The only thing that gave him hope and a little joy was thinking about the plane ticket to Hawaii sitting on his dresser at home. He was leaving everything behind; in just three days, he was going to pack up and leave for good. He thought for certain Hawaii was where he would find his happiness. He felt so disappointed that night because, after seeing my mom, he thought maybe he could find it with her instead.

Then something came over him; he was determined to try one more time. He had never really been a smooth-talker; words didn't come easy for him—not elegant ones anyway. It was no small thing for him to put himself out there; talking to my mom not once but twice that night was truly outside his comfort zone. So, when the party started to wind down, he approached her for the second time.

"May I walk you home?" he asked, with his entire body shaking.

"Sure," my mother replied sweetly, but still a little unsure.

Despite how awkward and bizarre my father had been that night, he still must have managed to make quite the impression. It was a short walk to her house, but it gave my dad enough time make a better, less weird, impression. They arrived at her house where she invited him in. They sat in her living room listening to music, one of her favorite things. Being serenaded by the musical stylings of "Meat Loaf" must have given my dad a third round of courage; he asked for her phone number, which to his surprise, she gave him.

He promptly called her the next day. As he dialed her number, the nervousness and anxiety was strong. When she answered, he felt a lump in his throat and butterflies in his stomach. He asked her on a proper date, and she agreed. Their first date was full of good conversation, laughter, and music. And my dad knew she was the one for him. He went home that night after their date and canceled his trip to Hawaii; he no longer needed a trip to search for happiness. He had already found it.

From there a relationship began. Even though they had found each other, their relationship was shaky and unstable. They had no faith to hold them up, no hope to see them through. It was far from the romantic fairy tale they both longed for. For years, they indulged in toxic behaviors, which left them feeling empty and left a negative impression on Brian—who was watching every move they made.

Although my dad wasn't always the greatest role model for Brian, he still loved him like he was his own son, and he treated my mom like she had never been treated before—like she had always wanted to be treated. My dad was exactly what she needed at the time, and he would be the one to lead her to the life she deserved. Even though they had found each other, their life still felt incomplete. My mom and dad still lived for no one but themselves, and living that way left their souls hollow. They filled most of their days with alcohol and drugs just trying to escape their past and pain. As great as their relationship felt, there was really nothing of substance behind it, and it was not built on anything solid. It was just a matter of time before it would crumble and their pasts would catch up with them.

My dad had a friend who often shared with my parents about the Gospel. He told of God's grace and His love, and that he could find everything he was looking for in Him. Chris would listen to his friend's words, and they would linger and enter into his thoughts from time to time, but he would just push those words aside.

One night, he and my mother threw a party. My dad woke up that morning in the living room; he had passed out on the couch. He sat up feeling foggy and empty as ever. He looked in front of him. The house was a mess and the coffee table was covered in beer bottles. In that moment, it hit him that this was not the life he wanted to be living. He felt empty and had enough. He wanted more than what was in front of him. He wanted to make a change. He remembered his friend's words from the day before, and right there in that moment, he knelt down by the beer-covered coffee table and gave his heart and life to Christ.

He wrestled with how to tell his beloved partner. He knew how she felt about such issues, so he knew it would not go well. But he was determined to change his life, and he couldn't do that without her.

Several days later, he found the courage to approach my mom. He walked up to her as she was lying on the floor of her bedroom smoking.

"I have something I need to talk to you about."

"What?"

"I have been feeling empty lately. The other morning, I woke up feeling it stronger than ever. Faith, believing in something bigger and more than this life has to offer, is something that has been floating in the back of my mind for a while now."

My mother sat up with a confused look on her face.

"And when I woke up, it was all of a sudden the only thing I was thinking. I am determined to make changes—no more drugs, no more drinking."

My mother smirked.

"I am going to stop going backward and start following God. And I need you and desperately want you to join me in my decision. I love you so much, but if you don't, I am not sure we can stay together if our paths are going in different directions."

Her reaction was not quite what he was hoping for, but it was pretty much what he expected. She stood up and laughed. "You are crazy. It is not for me."

She walked out of the room and slammed the door behind her. As my dad stood alone in their room, he started to wish he never told her. He started to wish he could take those words back because the fear of being without her was too much.

For weeks, their house was full of silence. My dad was heartbroken. He loved her so much, with all he had, so he waited, hoping she would change her mind. He didn't want to leave her or Brian, but if she wasn't willing to change, then he knew he had to. Life was awkward. Their relationship was strained greatly. They both thought it was over. One night, my mom was lying on the floor, staring at the ceiling indulging in pot, as she did most nights. Every night since my dad had told her of his decision, it was all she could think about, and with each passing day, her heart softened. Then something suddenly shifted in her heart. She looked at the joint in her hand and thought about how every night was full of meaningless and empty experiences. In that moment, she realized she was breaking the promise she made when she gave birth to Brian—that she would give him the life he deserved. She realized my dad was right. She decided she had lived enough years burdened down by pain and defining herself by her mistakes. She knew in the depths of her soul that she was meant for something greater than the life she was living. She knew there was healing out there for her and her son—she just had to find it. So at the age of twenty-four, she too gave her life over to God. My mother walked down the stairs to find my dad to tell him.

My dad watched her approach and thought, "This is it. She is leaving me." But he was shocked when he heard what came out of her mouth.

"You were right," she said. "We do need to change, and I am willing to change with you."

Together, my parents left everything they were and everything they had done and followed after a Love that would forever change them. And this time, my mother had finally found a Love that could cover all her pain and scars. In Christ, they found peace, love, forgiveness, and healing. In receiving Christ as her Savior, she discovered something amazing—grace. What she had done and what she had been through was washed clean and served a greater purpose than fueling her self-hate. God's grace had now covered all her faults and mistakes. Grace found her exactly where she was at, and it gave her a fresh start. My mother was no longer going to let the past and the pains define her; instead, she was going to let them make her stronger.

This change was not easy, and it didn't come overnight; she had to work really hard for it. She started off her new life by marrying the love of her life, Chris, on September 28, 1980. They had already begun their journey together, but now things were different; their love was built on something strong and that love could carry them through anything, that love could withstand anything that came its way. After getting married, my father officially adopted Brian. In their house, the term "stepson" was never used because in their hearts, Brian was his son.

Even though my mom had found everything she needed to become the woman she was meant to be and live the life she had always wanted to live, things still didn't come easy for her. She soon realized that life with God doesn't mean life will be easy; in some cases, it means life gets harder. My mother may have started following God, but she still lived in this world, a world full of suffering and pain, filled with humans who are imperfect and flawed, and she was one of them. Her past was still a burden on her heart as it was not erased, just forgiven. My mom's salvation didn't come with a promise that she would never face sorrow, but it did come with the promise that she would never have to go it alone again.

My mom knew that no matter what she faced, God was big enough to carry her through. And in the days and years to come, she held on to that promise with all of her heart. My parents came to the place in their marriage where they were ready to add to their family by having more children, but they soon realized that this process would not be an easy one. One of their worst fears came true the day the doctors told them it would be impossible for them to conceive a child. Even with this news, their faith gave them reason to believe that things might change, that one day, despite what they had been told, they would hold a baby of their own in their arms. For three years, they waited for their prayers to be answered. They daily called out to God for help, and while at times it seemed like He wasn't listening, they kept on praying. Then one night, they went to an evening church service, a special speaker was visiting their home church. They went up to the front for prayer. There was a hint of desperation in their voices as they asked the pastor to pray for them. The pastor laid hands on them and prayed for the baby my parents so desperately wanted. That night, God answered their prayers and they conceived their first child together.

Nine months later, on November 26, 1984, they welcomed me into their home and lives. They were filled with joy, and they always made sure I knew how much they loved me. And throughout my life, even when I didn't always feel it, I knew their love for me in the depths of my soul. When I was young, my mom and I were very close. For the first two years of my life, I never left her side. I loved her so much I couldn't stand to be without her, not even while I slept. Although my love exhausted my mother, she kept close. Three and a half wonderful years passed by and my parents were so happy, but still felt like something, or better yet someone, was missing. So in April 1988, when my mom gave birth to their son Matthew, they finally felt like they had found all that was missing. My parents' hearts were overflowing. They were told they could have no children together and now they were blessed with two. My mother loved her three children with all her heart. She never stopped praying for them and believing in them; she loved her children from their very first breath until her last. She now had everything she could ever want: a loving husband, three beautiful kids, and the best part, God was in the center of it all. But this was just the start. Life was just beginning. They had come so far, but their journey was far from over. Every tear they cried, every pain they experienced, and every regret they had was strengthening them for the times ahead. Their faith was soon going to be put to the test, and they were about to find out what they were really made of.

Letters from a Servant's Heart

(Entries from Kathleen's journal)

March 6, 1985
God has shown me that I need to ask for his strength daily. Maralee is keeping odd hours, and I don't get much rest. I must ask Him to help me to keep the eyes of my spirit open to the Risen Christ so that the drudgery that I face every day will not overtake me.

March 7, 1985
"No, in all these things we are more than conquerors through him who loved us." Romans 8:37 RSV

Sometimes things can and do come in between the devotional exercises of the soul and God and separate the soul and God and separate individual life from God; but none of them is able to wedge in between the love of God and the soul of the saint—My Utmost for His Highest

Sometimes I let things come between me and God, but He, Praise His Holy name, never lets anything come between His love for me.

March 12, 1985
God showed me today that I still have a critical spirit. I need to be patient with the faults of others, for they have to be patient with mine. Also I should abandon all to God, not to get anything back, but just because I want Jesus Christ, Himself.

March 14, 1985

Faith without works is dead; we need to exhibit our faith through our love for one another and meeting one another's needs. We are servants to whom we obey; we either obey our lust resulting in sin or we obey God resulting in righteousness. "Don't you know that when you offer yourselves to someone as obedient slaves, you are slaves of the one you obey—whether you are slaves to sin, which leads to death, or to obedience, which leads to righteousness?" Romans 6:16 NIV

March 15, 1985

I need to tell someone about Jesus. I need to start witnessing. Desiring to witness is a good thing, but I need to put it into action. Father, give me love and boldness to proclaim Your Gospel.

March 19, 1985

Today is not my day!! But praise the Lord, it is His!

November 2, 1985

I think God spoke to me. He said great and mighty things were about to happen soon. And that he would show me what to do and when the time came for me to do something, I would know what to do. (I had asked Him to help me make a difference in this world—for His glory.) He said to be obedient.

As I get rid of all the things that hinder my walk with God, and as I spend time in His Word and prayer, His desires will become a reality in my life. If I am to find an answer to anything I must seek the Lord's face as King David did. "David sought the face of the Lord," found in 2 Samuel 21:1 NIV

He didn't pray a simple prayer and that was it, God answered. He sought His face until he received an answer from Him. If I am troubled about something, I must learn to seek His face until I receive an answer directly from God.

Lord,
Things hurt. Help me to endure it and not lose heart or faint but help me to face up to it. I confess to You all my sins; they are so many. Please Lord make me clean and use me the way You intended to use me, especially in the area of music. From the time I was born again—restore unto me the joy of my salvation and renew a right spirit within me. Daily let me never forget who you are, Jesus, and what You have done for me. I pray for my family. For Chris, draw him closer to You; cause him to truly be the head of this home and let me let him. Show us Your will.

I pray for our children. I pray for You to cause them to be healthy and that You will always watch out for them wherever they go. Protect them from the evil one. Help them to know who they are in Christ. And help them to make right choices in their lives—to resist the enemy.

In Jesus' name,
Amen

October 1985
Jesus stands between myself and the judgment of God. I can come boldly to the throne of grace—I feel so unworthy. There are so many things in my life that ought not be there. But, praise be to God, I have an advocate to the Father my Lord and Savior, Jesus Christ. Every good work, no matter how small, is a testimony of God's saving power and a witness of His grace. I was down today because I felt like I wasn't good enough or important enough to make an impact on others, but God showed me that I was wrong. Every act of godliness, no matter how small, can manifest the glory of God and draw people to Christ.

July 1992
I will show you great mighty things, so many wondrous things.

Vision:

Jesus wrapped his arms around me and reaffirmed His love for me. He started walking me around with His arms around me and started to show me how he was going to do great and mighty things. There are the sick who need healing, people who are hungry for God, but do not know where to turn. Then I said, "Can I help, Lord?" And He answered, "As you abide in Me I will use you." Then we turned around and we were standing on a beach. Waves were coming in, the tide came up, and as the water got closer, I saw that it was not water at all but people, people who did not know God. Then the tide receded and went back again and just like when the tide goes back out again it leaves things on the beach, it left these people. Then I started to gather these things. I helped these people up and showed them the way to God.

November 11, 1992
Heavenly Father,

I thank You for Your Word in Solomon 4:16 NIV. The north wind awakening me to salvation, and I ask for the south wind to comfort me in my need. Forgive me my sin, I do not want to be like the woman who was forgiven but kept sinning, trampling the Son of God underfoot. "It's a dreadful thing to fall into the hands of the living God." Hebrews 10:31 NIV. But really what better place to be? Always pursue me, Lord. Don't let go. I need you. Help me in my singing ministry. Do Your will through me. Help me at home to praise and worship You. I know this is where it counts. Help me to shake this feeling that whatever I do is not enough for You. Help me to enjoy life; let it not always have to be a struggle for me. Give me wisdom in life. Amen

"I will show you great and mighty things, so many wondrous things."

Jesus [spoke to me and said]:

I am with you. Let Me hold you up. I will put a new song in your heart. I will give you joy where there has been no joy. I will give you peace where there has been no peace. You will be my bride, and I am preparing you. I will never let you go. I am married to you; I have made a covenant with you that will never be broken. There will be no lack in your life for I will meet your every need. For I love you with an everlasting love. A new love will spring forth in your heart, fresh, wonderful, and glorious like the dawning of a new day. I cast every evil work from your life and I bind the works of darkness and I release you from the chains of bondage and I say to you, "Rest, for I am keeping watch over your soul, you can rest now. I love you."

A lady from church asked me for forgiveness 'cause she thought I didn't like her. I have not opened my heart and my home enough to her—or to anyone for that matter. She spoke of me by saying I thought of myself as an island with no one to really talk to, and she was right. Sometimes I really have a pity party not thinking anyone really likes me—but then what kind of expression am I putting on with such a disposition?! People will think of me as unloving and uncaring! I must ask Jesus to help me not to seek for what love and care others can provide me, but what kind of love and care I can provide them. Lord, make me a servant!

CHAPTER THREE

Three Little Words

The task must be made difficult, for only the
difficult inspires the noble-hearted.
~ The Journals of Kierkegaard[1]

My mother lived more than half of her life for God. According to
her, it was one of the best decisions of her life. She still struggled
with her past. She often had nightmares about her abortion; she daily
wrestled with her relationship with her father, and it was not always
easy to make the daily choice to forgive him. She was often haunted
by her memories and past choices. Slowly she worked through her
pain and started to forgive the ones who had hurt her and most
importantly started to forgive herself.

Life in our family was good. We had our issues, but the family
was solid and strong. We attended church every Sunday together
and had family nights every Friday. We were happy. There was not
a lot of drama in our house. Then slowly things started to change.
My mother started acting differently. She started changing into a
person I didn't always recognize. It started with headaches, which
just kept getting worse. Then came the massive mood swings that

---

[1] *Søren Kierkegaard's Journals and Papers* Vol. 1, Indiana University Press,
(1967), edited and translated by Howard V. Hong and Edna H. Hong, p. 303.

were often filled with anger, hostility, and violence. She could feel herself changing and felt helpless to stop it. She was losing control and that scared her.

She knew in her heart that something wasn't quite right, she found herself saying things and doing things that she would never have done before. Her changes were slow at first, then became constant. She hated how she was treating her family but didn't know what to do to stop it. Her mind was not always her own. My mother's violent streak would often be taken out on us kids, especially me. Along with all her changes, she started to have great disdain for women and, unfortunately, her dislike extended to me too. Over time, her anger toward me became a constant. It was powerful and terrifying and it did not fade for many years.

I was sitting at my desk one morning in our living room and I must have done something to anger her. She marched over to me, grabbed me by my hair, and ripped me off my chair to the floor. She then began to drag me by my hair down the hallway. I remember screaming for help, knowing no one could hear me. I was so scared.

She had hurt me deeply; my heart was injured more than my body. I was somewhat used to her outbursts, the odd smack across my face that left a mark and me clenching my stinging cheek. Her tight grip on my shoulders whenever she would grab me out of anger. But that day seemed worse than the others. She always felt terrible afterward and apologized. But her repentance no longer mattered. Our wellbeing was in jeopardy and my dad was at a loss for what to do. My dad, scared for our safety and worried about his wife, greatly encouraged her to see a doctor; he made it clear he could no longer live this way. He needed to keep his children safe. So, not wanting to continue on with her behavior and with great fear of losing what she loved most, she made an appointment with her doctor. After a few visits, her family doctor then referred her to a specialist and after many weeks of tests and waiting, my mother got the answer to why she was changing. After my mother received her results, she returned home to tell my father. She walked through the front door, up the steps into the kitchen. She found my dad standing in front of the kitchen sink washing the dishes. He turned the water off, turned toward her, and asked, "What did the doctor say?"

"I have cancer," she answered with a smile on her face. "Brain tumors."

"Why are you smiling?"

"It's good news," she replied.

"How is that good news?" my dad said, with tear-filled eyes.

"It means I'm not crazy or a bad person. I'm just sick. It's not my fault. Now you don't have to leave me." My dad started to cry. All he could think to do was hold her.

After days had passed and they had some time to process the news, my parents decided it was time to tell us kids. They called us into the dining room and told us to take a seat at the dining room table. I slowly took a seat at the long scratched up wooden table where I spent a lot of my time. It was where I did my homework, it was where we celebrated every birthday, and it was where we ate dinner as a family. We had sat at this table many times before, but this time was different. We all sat in our seats quiet for a moment, then we heard our mom utter three little words that would change all of us forever.

"I have cancer," my mother said slowly and softly to us kids, as my dad stood behind her with his hands on her shoulders. Even during the worst of times, she managed to speak with softness and grace. We kids just sat there stunned and a little unsure of what exactly "cancer" meant. I was only ten and Matthew was just seven. We could not begin to fathom the road ahead. Brian was then twenty-one and those words were too much for him to take in. We couldn't quite grasp it. I remember just staring at my mom. She didn't look any different; she didn't seem sick. She looked like she always did. You would never guess that three golf-ball-sized tumors were now living in her brain. "Astrocytoma stage three" the doctors called it. And those technical words made it all the more terrifying. That was the exact moment everything changed; it would never be the same again. Over the years, the family I knew and loved got lost. My mother slowly lost herself, my dad's strength dimmed, and Matthew's and my hearts would never be full.

The plan for the next year was laid out carefully. We were going to be spending a lot of time apart while my mother got the treatment she needed. All of a sudden, life seemed to go by so quickly, and we were powerless to slow it down. It was like a whirlwind filled with doctor visits, surgeries, and treatments. Three months after the diagnosis, she left for Vancouver. It was a bigger city, and it had better hospitals that could provide her with the best care. There she could get the treatments she desperately needed. For six months, we spent a lot of time away from our parents as our mom underwent aggressive treatments, such as chemotherapy and radiation. She also had to endure multiple surgeries to try to remove the tumors. We would go months at a time without seeing our mom. We missed her terribly. We wrote her letters and drew her pictures often, and she was faithful in phoning us once in the morning to tell us to have a good day and once in the evening before bed to say I love you and goodnight. Even though we loved hearing her voice and reading her letters, it just wasn't the same as having her home with us. My dad would often go to be with my mom for support and so that she wouldn't be lonely. For the first six months of my mom being away, we hopped around from our home to our aunt's to our grandparents'. Things for us felt so unstable, and it was taking its toll on us. We knew they had to go away and that it was for the best, but there was also a part of us that didn't want to be left behind. We were hurt. We had outbursts and bouts of crying because we missed our mother so much. But to balance things out and make things a little easier, my mom would come back home occasionally to see us. It was never for long, usually just for the weekend. It was better than nothing, but it was also hard having to always say goodbye. Even though we were small, we were afraid that every goodbye might be the last. One day my dad decided to take us to Vancouver to visit our mom. The drive to Vancouver felt like it took forever. On the way, our car started acting up. After hours of having problems with the car, my dad took it into a mechanic, and he told my dad that if he hadn't brought the car in, the engine would have most likely exploded. We waited four hours for the car to be fixed. I cried the whole time and just wanted to get to my mom. What was supposed to be an eight-hour car ride turned into a fourteen-hour ordeal. By the time we arrived in Vancouver, we were exhausted and drained from the trip. But the moment we saw our mother's face and she held us in her arms, we no longer cared about the bad day we'd had; in that moment, she made everything better. She was our home. When we saw her, everything felt steady again. I remember it feeling so good to finally be spending time with my mommy. I have this memory of just me and her, watching TV while she painted my nails. It is a small memory, but to this day, I hold on to it dearly. Matthew and I learned early on to hold on to the small, good things we experienced, and in times of struggle, the small things didn't seem so small anymore. I remember a day we were sitting on a couch, and she pulled us close, one kid under each of her arms. She pulled out a big box and slowly took off the lid. As I peeked inside, Matthew and I smiled. Inside, the box was filled with the pictures we had drawn for her and the letters we had written.

"I keep them all," she said. "They help me feel better."

Over the course of our visit, our parents made sure we had a good time. They wanted to take the crummy situation and turn it around. They took us to a bunch of different places—the Aquarium, the Science Centre, shopping, and out for dinner. The four days we spent together as a family were amazing, and for a short time, it made us forget our situation. We were just happy. There were moments when I would forget that my mom was sick. I forgot the pain. I forgot the fear. And I could have lived in that place forever. There I could pretend everything was back to normal; I could pretend everything was okay. The problem with living in that place for too long was that it made going back to reality all the more excruciating.

Mom made us dinner most nights, and for a time, things felt

normal and safe. We would sit around the dinner table together, and it felt like home if only for a moment. That trip let us go back in time to before the cancer; it gave us a glimpse into the past where we were happy and had nothing to fear. When it came time to say goodbye, our hearts tore. Once again, we were uprooted from what we loved the most. We did not want to go back home without our mom. It really wasn't home without her in it.

The six months really took a toll on my mother's body and her mind. She did radiation for two months and had daily doses of steroids. At the end of the first round of steroids, the doctors advised my mom to do another round. The first round was so intense that she refused. She bluntly told the doctors that she would rather be shot in the head then go through that again. She stopped with the steroids and continued with just the radiation and additional surgeries. As the days went on, she started to lose her hair, although half of it was already shaved from her surgeries. Before she was sick, my mother had the most beautiful hair. It was dark brown, thick, and curly. It was long, past her shoulders. She loved her hair. Now she was losing one of the things she liked most about herself. I can't imagine how insecure she must have felt. The side effects from the treatments were intense. Hair loss was one of the minor effects my mother experienced compared to everything else she endured. She experienced stomach problems, sleeplessness, fatigue, memory loss, intense mood swings, weight gain, burns on her body, swelling, and seizures among many other things. Those six months were long, and she tried so hard to keep busy. She pushed through how she was feeling and tried to fill up her days. She went out almost every day—no matter how she felt. She went out for meals and movies. She did a lot of shopping. But she spent most of her time visiting with people in the cancer lodge and talking on the phone to her friends and family. I believe she was too scared to slow down because if she did, she might feel the extent of her pain—and not just the pain that came from her illness, but the pain that came from the fear of what was ahead. She also spent a lot of her time writing in her journals. She found it therapeutic and helpful. It helped her organize her thoughts and say what was deep in her heart. She wrote daily about her feelings and what bothered her, but on a deeper level, she wrote prayers to God. She wrote about how she could improve herself and explored all the things God was telling her. She would write pages and pages on how she could and should love others. Here she was, sicker than she had ever been, and instead of complaining, she focused on others and how she could be a better person. Her journal was also filled with scriptures. She found verses that applied to what she was thinking or feeling. She would write them down, study them, and dwell on them.

During my mother's treatments, she didn't come home much. I remember one of the only times she returned home, we were more than thrilled to see her again. The day she was supposed to arrive, we waited eagerly by the door, sitting on the entryway stairs. We had made a welcome home sign and hung it on the door. But when the door opened, we were stunned by what we saw. She was physically different than the mom who had left us and even different from the last time we saw her. This time, we could see the sickness all over her face. She had become almost unrecognizable. She had gained over 100 pounds. She had a black eye—a side effect from the treatments. Half of her hair was missing, and she had staples all across her head from her surgeries. At first, we were taken aback by her changed appearance, but she slowly approached us and whispered, "It's all right." She brought us close and explained all the changes, then held us in her arms, and we were no longer afraid. As her family, we could see past the sickness and see her true beauty. We did not care what she looked like; we were just glad she was home.

About a month after that visit, she came home for good. With our mother home, things were better, but certainly not easy. Every day was a battle. It was us against the cancer, and at times, it seemed like we were being defeated. Soon after she returned home, my mom went to the hairdresser and had her head shaved. I think she just wanted, and needed, a fresh start. My mom was now completely bald but still completely beautiful. She wrapped beautiful scarves around her head and wore hats when she was out in public; she wouldn't even let her friends see her bald head. But at home, she felt safe and comfortable enough to just be herself.

With our dad at work, Matthew and I were left to watch over our mom when we weren't in school. This newfound responsibility forced us to grow up quickly.

Soon the cancer started causing our mom to have seizures, one or two almost every day. If we were around our mother when she had a seizure, it was our job to tell her four words, and after the seizure was over, we had to ask her to repeat those words back to us. The doctors wanted to know how conscious and aware she was during her seizures. Words cannot even begin to describe how scary it is to see your mother fall to the ground with no control over her own body. I was scared to death that she'd stop breathing, that she'd hurt herself. Our hearts would drop every time we walked into a room and found our mom shaking on the ground. When my mom started having seizures, we were just eleven and eight years old. Witnessing our mother flailing helplessly on the ground was like living a nightmare. The worst part was the look on her face. She would just stare without blinking, saliva dripping down her chin. You could tell she was frightened by the way she would grip our hands tightly. When she would have a seizure, I would hold her hand in mine. With my other hand, I would gently stroke her cheek while whispering to her that everything would be all right. Then afterward, I would hold her in my arms. Every time, I swear you could hear my heart break, and when the seizure would stop and she would see her terrified kids with tears running down their faces holding her hands, you could hear hers break as well.

My family and I did this every day for almost eleven years. We tried not to show how afraid and helpless we were, but we were kids, and the pain of it all seeped out of us. No matter how often she had seizures—and she had well over 1,000 in her life—it never became normal, and we never got used it.

Three years after my mom was diagnosed, she and my dad headed back to Vancouver for a routine MRI scan. The results of her scan were remarkable. They were clean; there was no sign of the cancer and there was nothing left but scar tissue. The doctors were in disbelief and thought maybe something had malfunctioned. But it was no mistake—our mother was in remission, and she stayed that way for seven years. She started doing much better, and for a short time, things were looking up. She could not keep this miracle to herself. She shouted the news of her healing from the top of her lungs. She was the kind of person who needed to share her life with others. She used her own life to share her faith and to connect with others. Most days, my mother felt a lot of emotional pain, but she knew how to recognize the good. In fact, her pain provided the opportunities to help and bless those around her.

We spent years in celebration of her recovery. Everything felt more secure, but life never really went back to the way it used to be. She still had seizures, and she had her bad days, but overall, things were good. After some time had passed, we began to notice more changes in our mom's behavior. She started to become forgetful. She started having difficulty understanding the simplest things. All these changes filled us with worry. We felt like we had just gotten our mom back, and we could not bear to think we may lose her again. So we ignored it for a while, thinking and hoping she would return to her old self, but when she didn't, when it reached the point where she was getting worse and not better, my dad nervously took her to the doctor to find out what was going on.

Life took yet another turn when the doctor told my parents something that instantly broke their hearts.

Nine years after my mother was diagnosed, I found myself exactly where we started, sitting at that long wooden dining room table being told something that would change our family and our lives even more

My dad told us that all the surgeries, the aggressive treatments, and all the seizures she endured were causing her brain to deteriorate.

The doctor said that within five years, our mom would enter a vegetative state. We were told that we would watch her slowly fade away until there was nothing left. And that is what eventually happened. She would lose her ability to walk, to feed herself, to speak, to clothe herself, to go to the bathroom and to bathe on her own. She would come to depend on her family to do all those things for her. We started to dread each day that got us close to that gloomy fate. We sat at that table quiet for what seemed to be an eternity. After Matthew and I were told the news, we went for a walk together around our neighborhood with our arms linked together. We didn't talk much on our walk; you could only hear the quiet sound of our crying.

After my mom learned what would happen to her, she pleaded with my dad, "Don't leave me. Don't put me in a home. No matter what happens, don't ever leave me alone."

My dad took her hand, looked deep into her eyes, and said, "Let's make a pact. I won't put you in a home if you promise to never leave me in your mind. Don't leave me. Don't forget me."

"Deal," my mom replied with a smile.

Just as they thought one fight was ending, another began. It was a lot to grasp, but no matter what we were about to face, we were not alone.

Letters of a Fighter

(Entries from Kathleen's journal)

November 1992

I pray again Lord for my marriage. It seems that all these things are happening again to keep me and Chris apart. The eye infection, sores, and fatigue. Lord Your Word said that you took all our sickness and diseases, and I cling to Your healing for my body in Jesus' name. I rebuke the spirit of infirmity and tell it to go in Jesus' name!

May 29, 1996

I was taken to get an MRI scan at 7:30 a.m. I can't have anything to eat all day. I have surgery scheduled for 1 p.m. Everything is going very well. The anesthesiologist came to see me this morning to explain things. He says I'll have to have a bigger IV in my arm and my neck … yuck! I am feeling pretty tired, probably just from the sleeping pills I took last night. Jesus is ever close to me and Jesus is still Lord! I'll be getting my head shaved a bit sometime this morning.

June 6, 1996

Went shopping and then went home—couldn't wait to get home! I missed Maralee and Matthew so much! We made it home around 8 p.m. Jack [stepdad] and Mom did a wonderful job watching over the kids. Maralee cried a lot and was quite upset about me, it was hard on Mom, but she got over it as soon as I got home. A lot of people brought over meals I could freeze and use at our convenience. God Bless them every one! People showed a lot of love and concern.

June 11, 1996

Tried calling home in the morning, but they weren't home. I miss them so much! I keep seeing Maralee's and Matthew's faces and imagining holding them in my arms again, and just being with them.

Cried a lot this morning, I know the Lord is with me and that He has everything under his control, but I feel a little apprehensive about everything. And I miss Chris and the kids so much my heart aches. I hope I can see them all soon! I called Chris around lunch; he and the kids just got home from camping; they had a good time. At one point at night around the fire Matthew was acting a little funny and finally told the truth and said he just wanted to go home. Chris said they were having such a good time and could not understand why he wanted to go home. Matthew said it was so he could smell his mommy ... SOB!

Good news! I just phoned Chris and he booked four nights at the Easter Seal House! I can't wait for them to arrive even as I write this!

June 12, 1996

I expected the kids and Chris around 1 p.m., but their car broke down twice. They didn't get to the lodge until 7:30. It was wonderful to see them again! We took the kids to Science World; we all had such a good time together. We went to McDonald's for lunch and Burger King for dinner.

June 14, 1996

We just hung out together, went to the mall for a bit, and came back to the Easter Seal House, and I cooked supper for everyone.

We went to the Aquarium for the day and again had a wonderful day together. It was pretty hot and the kids were disappointed they didn't get splashed by the killer whales. We had supper at Wendy's and then said our goodbyes. That was hard. Maralee cried.

June 16, 1996

Good news! Chris and the kids stayed another night! There was a mix up at the Easter Seal House. We just spent the day together, and I cooked supper again. Chris drove me back to the Lodge, and we said goodbye again!!

Chris and the kids showed up at 6:30 a.m. to say goodbye again!! For the third time we said goodbye! They made it home at 6:30.

June 28, 1996

I went to Victory Church and an older lady came up to me and was asking my advice on how I am dealing with things in this situation. So I was able to help her. I told her the things I prayed for and scriptures to stand on every day. She had something wrong with her back and she just wanted to know what she could do. It was wonderful to be able to help a sister in the Lord.

June 29, 1996

I started to notice quite a bit of hair loss. Wrote a letter, read, and then slept most of the day.

Found more hair on my pillow today, had to shake my pillow off outside, then clumps of it came out in my comb and hands.

June 31, 1996

Tried some wigs on this morning — yuck! So I took some turbans for now.

July 30, 1996

While I was worshipping God this morning, He showed me that He is not only my "Rock," but that He is my "shield" as well—Shield me from negative effects of the radiation.

Even So

Aug 1, 1996
More hair is falling out, and I feel like going to sleep right after breakfast. Had a shower and packed after supper. Lord, just help me sleep through the night!! I'm going home tomorrow!!

August 2, 1996
When I got home, there were balloons on the basketball hoop and a sign on the door welcoming me home. It was good to be home again! We ordered pizza and just enjoyed being with one another.

August 3, 1996
Still at home and enjoying being here with my family. Chris had repainted part of the kitchen and did some repairs and even put a bi-fold door on the pantry! He also did some work on the bathroom, fixed the outside wall, and painted the walls and the tiles. He put a drawer under the vanity and a shelf above the toilet!

Chris rented Sense and Sensibility for me and I enjoyed it immensely!

We were in our way to church, but we had to turn around and come back home because we had a fight. The devil is trying to get us any way that he can!

August 4, 1996
Showed up to church 15 minutes late, but we had a good time. The Pastors prayed for us after the service. One thing we were reminded of was that if we are not in agreement God was limited in working in our lives. We took the kids to McDonald's after church and then stopped off at Aunt Becky's to see if things were still all right about the kids staying with her while Chris drove me back to Vancouver, and they were.

Went home and did laundry and started to pack.

August 6, 1996
Got to the Lodge in Vancouver around 11 p.m. last night. Went to the clinic to let them know I was there, and they took me in for treatment right away. My appointment with the doctor went well. She seemed to be more concerned and sensitive about things. She didn't seem to think that the burn on my head would get any more painful, even though it may get red.

August 9, 1996
Had a nap in the morning and afternoon. Feel very tired today.
Selected three turbans at the clinic today.
After this manner therefore pray ye:
Our Father which art in heaven, Hallowed be thy name.
Thy kingdom come, Thy will be done on Earth, as it is in heaven.
Give us this day our daily bread.
And forgive us our debts, as we forgive our debtors.
And lead us not into temptation, but deliver us from evil:
For thine is the kingdom, and the power, and the glory, for ever.
Amen. Matthew 6:9-13 KJV

CHAPTER FOUR

Faithfulness

Faith is unseen but felt,
Faith is strength when we feel there is none,
Faith is hope when all seems lost.
~ Catherine Pulsifer

Quickly, my mother was drifting away. She was starting to lose control of her body and mind, but even so, she never gave up. Although she sometimes wavered and struggled with what might become of her, she never lost heart and she never lost hope.

When it came to my mother's faith, she could be quite outspoken. She took the Bible literally and clung to every word. She was certain in her beliefs and confident in her faith. Before becoming a Christian, she was unsure and broken. But her faith had transformed her. It made her bold, it made her new, and it made her brave. She deeply loved people and sometimes out of that love, she would express concern and share her strong opinions with people on how they were living their lives. Sometimes people were grateful, but often, they were offended by my mother's words, which often resulted in her feeling lonely and hurt. She felt a call so strong to share the faith she had found, to share about the God who changed everything for her. Her faith and her love for God were just too great, too important to keep to herself. She loved people so deeply she just wanted them to have what she had. When she saw people hurt, when she saw the pain all over their faces, she just desperately wanted them to find the healing she found. Over time, she adjusted the way she did things and tried to be more tactful in the way she spoke to others. She stopped preaching and started sharing her past and her experiences instead, in hopes that she would help someone.

The differences are many when it comes to how my mother expressed her faith and how I express mine. My mother's passion was so strong it seeped out of her. I tend to be more subtle and laid-back when it comes to my faith. I try to let my words be few and let my actions be many and let my life speak for itself. When I read my mother's words, I don't always understand her passion and intensity. But the faith that comes through in her words hits me every time. Even though I don't talk like she does or pray like she does, I want to have faith like hers. Her unbridled passion gave her a hope, a peace, and a purpose—all things I long for.

My mother had this amazing faith right from the start and she never let go of that. It is what carried her through; it is what gave her strength when she alone was too weak to carry on.

When my mom first got the news that she was sick, there is no doubt she was scared. It showed in her eyes even though she tried her best to hide it. She had no idea where this road would take her or how her story would end. She didn't know how sick she would get, or if she would make it to her children's next birthdays.

But there is one thing she did know: she knew that no matter what happened to her, God was in control. She knew He was strong enough and powerful enough to heal her from all sickness and all pain. And because of that, she knew that no matter what happened, she would be okay. I am still baffled by her ability to completely surrender everything.

The most common question my mom was asked was, "What if God doesn't heal you?"

Every time she would reply without hesitation, "Whether He heals me or not, I will still love my God."

She would say that, just like the story in the Bible of Shadrach, Meshach, and Abednego, you could throw her in the fire; *even so* she would still serve her God.

She was so certain that God's plan was the right one, no matter what that would mean for her. Nothing could happen to her that would change how she felt about Him. She felt she would stay loyal to the very end, and as time went on, she proved that to be true.

There were many people who crossed her path who doubted her faith and whose words could have discouraged or derailed her, but she tried to never let anyone's opinions get to her. One day at church, a woman approached her and said that the reason she was sick was because she did not have enough faith, that she was too sinful. She could have taken great offense or gotten mad and stormed off, but instead she looked kindly into the lady's eyes, smiled and said, "Okay, thank you for your opinion. Can you tell me how I can have more faith?"

She knew she had faith and nobody's opinion could change the truth. She also knew there is always room for growth and that maybe she could do better. Even though that woman's words hurt her, she was willing to listen in case there was something she could learn. Some people would tell my parents that if she were to die, it would be their fault because they did not pray or believe hard enough. That lie was told to them repeatedly and would even come from those closest to them. At first it was easy to brush off those words, but the more they heard it, the harder it was to disregard. Even though there was no truth to it, they sometimes worried that they did not have enough faith.

Faith was important to my mother. As the years went by, it often felt like it was all she had. In the beginning of her sickness, she looked my dad right in the eyes and made a threat he would never forget. She said, "If you ever lose faith, when I die, I will come back and kick your butt." It was the greatest threat he had ever heard.

People often mistook my mother's faith for stubbornness or

denial. When my mom started her first round of chemotherapy, the doctor told her that she would most likely become very ill. My mother's response to this was a simple, "No, I won't." They argued back and forth about this with the doctor eventually giving up. The chemo never did affect my mom like she was told it would. Halfway through her treatment, my mom visited her doctor unannounced to boast about how right she was. She walked through the clinic doors, walked past the receptionist, and into the doctor's office where he was with another patient. My mom shouted, "I'm not sick! I told you!" and proceeded to do a dance in front of the doctor and a total stranger. The doctor shocked but pleased smiled, my mom grinned back turned around and walked out.

As her sickness progressed, she started to find it difficult to read. She found she could no longer understand the words on a page. My mom had been a diligent reader of the Bible. It was a daily part of her life before she got sick, and she was not going to give it up. Her great faith and so much of who she was had been rooted in her love of the Bible. So, every night, even after she couldn't read, she would get in bed and open her Bible and stare at the pages—even though she couldn't always understand the words on the page—just hoping that some of what she was looking at would become clear to her. The memory of her lying in bed under the covers with her side lamp on and her Bible open on her lap, staring longingly at it with a slight smile on her face is still clear in my mind and one of the most beautiful things I have ever seen.

My mom taught us the importance of being faithful to God and to each other. When the time came that my mom needed full-time supervision at home, it became clear to me that I would be the one to take care of her. Halfway through grade eleven, I dropped out of high school to be home with my mom, to watch over her, and to be there in case of an emergency. Too many times we would come home and find my mother lying on the floor; she would have a seizure, fall to the ground, and lay there for hours waiting for us to come home. My dad had to work and my brother was too young. It seemed like the only solution. I tried homeschooling for a few months, but over time, school faded away; it just sort of got lost in the shuffle. I did less and less work until I was doing none. It wasn't a conscious choice, it just stopped being important. In comparison it didn't seem to matter. I had no one to help me with the work and no one to hold me accountable. It seemed I wasn't the only one who didn't care about it anymore. When I let it go, no one ever asked me about it again.

My dad and I became her full-time caretakers. Although we loved being there for her and helping her through, that also meant we had front-row seats to watching her slip away from us, becoming this person we didn't know. Her deterioration was very slow. We got to see every painful second of it.

She started out forgetful and would become easily confused. She would often get her words jumbled up and lose her train of thought. Then after a couple of years went by, anger set in. She once again turned mean and violent and was constantly mad at everything and everyone. We knew that anger was an inevitable side effect, but that didn't make it any easier to handle or accept. There were times where I was genuinely afraid of her. Where I was terrified of my own mom.

A few more years went by and she became more and more like a child. She would throw temper tantrums because she didn't want her teeth brushed or her hair combed. She needed constant supervision and became fully dependent on others.

But along with the lows came some beautiful highs. After the anger stage faded away, my mother became so full of joy. She was constantly laughing, and her laugh was contagious. You could not help but smile when my mother was in the room. The joy she had was rooted so deep it overflowed her soul.

My mother developed the innocence and faith of a child, and she loved unconditionally like a child. She had this unbelievable courage that would allow her to completely live in the moment, without caring what anyone thought of her. She loved to praise God. It didn't matter where she was or what she was doing. We could be watching a sitcom and she would stand up and start singing, "Jesus, Jesus!" She would praise Him every time she heard "O Canada." Everyone could be staring at her, but she didn't care. For years, her favorite song was "I've Got the Joy," a children's song that I sang in Sunday school as a little girl. Those simple lyrics became her life song.

"I've got the joy, joy, joy, joy down in my heart. I've got the peace that passes understanding down in the depths of my heart, 'cause I'm so happy, so very happy I've got the love Jesus in my heart."

She would sing that song almost every day. But she didn't just sing it—she lived it. She had a joy deep within and a peace that I envied. The love and faith she had in Jesus was all she needed, and it gave her the foundation for her joy. With everything she faced and was still facing, she was truly happy because true joy is bigger than fear and circumstance.

Most people don't ever find the true joy my mom found. And most people haven't gone through what my mom endured. If you have joy planted deep within your heart and soul, no one and no bad circumstance can uproot it. Happiness is often based on your circumstances, but joy comes in spite of it. It sustains when happiness is absent. My mother's joy was not based on whether or not she was healed, it wasn't dependent on other people, it was based on who she was created to be, her purpose, and in the act of loving God, her family and those around her. She could find it in every song she sang and every word she prayed. Her joy was found in things that could not be lost or taken. This world can take a lot from us. It can take the people we love, the life we live but it can't take the love we gave, the work we've done, the laughter, or the honor of just being someone's partner, parent, or child. She could be right in the middle of the grimmest of places, and she could still find the joy in it. Her joy was not wrapped up in anyone or anything. Because if those things were gone then her joy would be gone too. Her joy was found in her actions and she could rest peacefully in it, no matter what came next, no matter the changes that were to come, nothing could undo it. It shows your true character, what you are truly made of when you can keep the faith and joy through the worst of times. At times, the cancer and sickness did get to my mother. There were days when it consumed her and made everything seem dark, but even at the end of her darkest days, her faith was still there—and so was her joy. She didn't always feel them, but she knew it to be true. My mother had built her life upon a solid foundation made of love, hope, joy, and faith, and no matter how many tears she shed, her foundation stood strong. It is what stopped her from crumbling. Her circumstances were what she had to go through; they were not who she was.

My mother was not a perfect woman. She was flawed. Her illness often caused her to lose control. In an instant, she would go from a mom who was loving and kind to a monster who I was greatly afraid of. In the moments where she was herself, I saw her make amends, I saw her try hard to change, I would hear her promises to be do better next time. But her illness was strong. She wrestled daily with who she truly was and who her sickness was making her to be.

My mother was a beautiful woman, but it was the beautiful way she lived her life that caught everybody's attention. Her life was not always pretty. At times it was even hard to look at. But no matter how many times she failed or unwillingly broke those promises to do better, she never stopped trying. Every time her sickness knocked her down, she got back up. She laid her mistakes and failures down and then she tried again. She taught me living beautifully doesn't mean living perfectly.

Eventually her sickness started showing in her appearance: her hair was thinning, she weighed approximately ninety pounds, her complexion was pale, she lost some height, and the changes in her body caused her skin to lose its elasticity. Looking at her face, you could tell she was tired and worn, but despite all of these changes, the beauty of her heart shone through. Her inside overtook her outside. Her faith and pure joy made her stunning to everyone who laid eyes on her. With every laugh, with every dance, with every honest word, her beauty became more intensified. One of the many lessons I have learned is that beauty is more precious and stunning when it is real, honest, raw and comes from the depths of who you are.

Letters of Faith

(Journal entries written while Kathleen
was in the cancer clinic in 1996)

In the name of the Lord, I exercise authority over this body of mine. Sickness and disease, I refuse to allow you to stay. This body, this house belongs to God. It is a temple of God. You have no right to trespass on God's property. Now get out! You leave my body. I've got authority over you. You know it, I know it, and God knows it. I hold fast to what I have. I am keeping my healing!

Brain tumor; remove yourself from my body, in Jesus' name. You cannot live in me, you cannot kill me, and you can't even stay in my body. Go into the depths of the sea. Thank You, Lord, for removing it from my body. Thank You that my brain is normal, in Jesus' name.

"Therefore everyone who hears these words of mine and puts them into practice is like a wise man who built his house on the rock. The rain came down, the streams rose, and the winds blew and beat against that house; yet it did not fall, because it had its foundation on the rock." Matthew 7:24-25 NIV

"He himself bore our sins" in his body on the cross, so that we might die to sins and live for righteousness; "by his wounds you have been healed." 1 Peter 2:24 NIV

He personally bore our sins in His own body to the tree, like an altar and offered Himself on it, that we might die, cease to exist to sin and live to righteousness, By His wounds you have been healed.

"Surely he took up our pain and bore our suffering, yet we considered him punished by God, stricken by him, and afflicted. But he was pierced for our transgressions, he was crushed for our iniquities; the punishment that brought us peace was on him, and by his wounds we are healed," Isaiah 53:4-5 NIV

Surely He has borne our grief, sickness, weakness and distress and carried our sorrows and pain of punishment, yet we ignorantly considered

Him stricken and smitten and afflicted by God as if by leprosy. But He was wounded for our transgressions, He was bruised for our guilt and iniquities; the chastisements needful to obtain peace and well-being for us were upon Him and with the stripes that wounded Him we are healed and made whole.

What if some were unfaithful? Will their unfaithfulness nullify God's faithfulness? Not at all! Let God be true, and every human being a liar. As it is written: "So that you may be proved right when you speak and prevail when you judge," Romans 3:3-4 NIV

What if some did not believe and were without faith? Do their lack of faith and their faithfulness nullify and make ineffective and void the faithfulness of God and His fidelity to His word? By no means! Let God be found true though every human being false and a lair.

"If you declare with your mouth, "Jesus is Lord," and believe in your heart that God raised him from the dead, you will be saved. For it is with your heart that you believe and are justified, and it is with your mouth that you profess your faith and are saved," Romans 10:9-10 NIV

If you read in the Greek, "saved" pertains to healing as surely as the new birth—the Greek word "sozo" which is translated "saved" literally means "to be made sound, to be delivered from every form of sickness and danger, both temporal and eternal."

It was the will of the Lord to bruise Him; He has put him to grief and made Him sick — IF it was the will of God to bruise Him and make Him carry our sickness, how can it be the will of God to bruise us and make us carry those same sicknesses again? It can't be! That would be a travesty of divine justice.

Thank you Lord for Isaiah 53:4-5—That You have purchased my healing the same time as you purchased my redemption from sin. So health is available to me just as Your salvation in Galatians 5:6 tells me that faith works by love, so help me to operate in love and put love into action.

"Therefore I tell you, whatever you ask for in prayer, believe that you have received it, and it will be yours," Mark 11:24 NIV

Lord, help me not to go by what I feel or see, but just simply believe what You say—when I pray.

"And whatever we ask we receive from Him, because we keep His commandments and do the things that are pleasing in His sight," 1 John 3:22 KJV

Help me Lord to lead a life free from habitual sin and rebellion so I can have confidence in my heart before You all my life in the good and the bad.

"And whenever you stand praying, if you hold anything against anyone, forgive him that your Father in heaven may also forgive you your trespasses." Mark 11:25-26 NKJV

"In this the children of God and the children of the devil are manifest: Whoever does not practice righteousness is not of God, nor is he who does not love his brother. For this is the message that you heard from the beginning, that we should love one another, not as Cain who was of the wicked one and murdered his brother. And why did he murder him? Because his works were evil and his brother's righteous. Do not marvel, my brethren, if the world hates you. We know that we have passed from death to life, because we love the brethren. He who does not love his brother abides in death. Whoever hates his brother is a murderer, and you know that no murderer has eternal life abiding in him. By this we know love, because He laid down His life for us. And we also ought to lay down our lives for the brethren. But whoever has this world's goods, and sees his brother in need, and shuts up his heart from him, how does the love of God abide in him? My little children let us not love in word or in tongue, but in deed and in truth. And by this we know that we are of the truth, and shall assure our hearts before Him. For if our heart condemns us, God is greater than our heart, and knows all things," 1 John 3:10-20 [NKJV].

Here's how you tell the difference between God's children and the devil's children: the one who won't practice righteous ways isn't from God, nor is the one who won't love brother or sister. A simple test ... If you see some brother or sister in need and have means to do something about it but turn a cold shoulder and do nothing, what happens to God's love? It disappears. You made it disappear. Let's not just talk about love; let's practice real love. This is the only way we'll know we're living truly, living in God's reality. It's also the way to shut down debilitating self-criticism even when there is something to it. For God is greater than our worried hearts and knows more about us than we do ourselves we're bold and free before God! We're able to stretch out our hands and receive what we asked for because we are doing what he said, doing what pleases him. If anyone boasts "I love God" and goes right on hating his brother or sister he is a liar. If he won't love the person he can see how can he love the God he can't see? The command we have from Christ is blunt: Loving God includes loving people. You've got to love both.

CHAPTER FIVE

Words Fail, Music Speaks

I would wrap the notes around me like a blanket.
When life was too heavy the melody would take me
away and when I missed you too much, the harmony
brought you back to me, even just for a moment.
~ Maralee Mason

My mom was a woman of many passions, but there was one in particular she loved the most: singing.

Even when she was a teenager and life for her was really rough, she would sing. At seventeen, she joined a band and was the lead singer. Everyone who came to hear them play was captivated by her amazing voice. Her brothers would come to hear her sing, and they were so proud of her. Her voice was a light in the darkness.

Her voice was filled with love, soul, and passion. She didn't just use her singing as a hobby, but as a tool as well. My mom would use a song to touch somebody's heart, and to sing her children to sleep. She especially loved to use her voice for singing praises to her God. It didn't matter if she was on stage leading worship on Sunday or in her house alone, she just loved to sing to the Heavens.

When my brothers and I were little, Mom would teach us all kinds of songs. In school, she would direct the choirs. She would even get asked to sing on the local TV station. When we would go on long trips, we were that weird family that would sing at the top of our lungs even if the windows were rolled down. Music was a big part of my mom and our family.

There were many wonderful things about my mother, but her singing voice is what she was known for. Now I don't mean she could just carry a tune; my mother could really sing. Her voice had the power to stop you in your tracks. You could feel every word she sang deep in your bones. My mom's voice had the power to change our family, and one day, it did. I was a little girl, and my parents hit a rough patch in their marriage. They had many hard times throughout their marriage, but this time it seemed worse than the others.

Their love was getting put to the test, and they fought their hardest to make it to the other end. In spite of the rough times they were facing, they took us kids on a family vacation to Edmonton, Alberta. On our trip, we all went shopping at West Edmonton Mall. As we were walking around, my mother spotted a recording booth in the center of the mall. In this booth, you could record a song and they would give you a copy and play it throughout the entire mall. My mom got in the booth and she did what she did best—she sang. Before she began recording, she dedicated the song to her husband. She went on to sing a song called, "I Just Never Say It Enough," a song about saying the most important words to the one you love the most before it's too late. That gesture changed everything for my parents. When we got back home, my older brother secretly took a copy of the recording and brought it to the local radio station. They listened to it and instantly fell in love.

Shortly after, while my mom was sitting in the living room, my brother ran in and turned on the radio while yelling for everyone to join him. To my mom's surprise, she heard her voice. We all sat shocked that we were hearing our mom's voice on the radio. The whole family sat quietly with smiles on our faces, listening to every beautiful word. When the song ended, we all got up and danced around the living room in celebration of my mom's radio debut. After that, the local radio station played her song for more than a month. She became a local celebrity. She had a radio interview, where they talked about her beloved husband and how she sang the song for him. She even spoke directly to him, saying, "I love you, honey, and all you who work with him can eat your heart out." Our family had their picture in the newspaper along with a story about my mom. The phone was ringing off the hook with people wanting a copy of her song. And now everyone knew what I knew: the true love that my parents shared and that my mom had the most beautiful voice in the entire world.

After my mom was diagnosed and some time had passed, she started to lose her singing voice among other things. Singing was something that she loved dearly. It was a gift she cherished. Music was how she expressed herself and it was how she would share the gospel with others. But now suddenly it was gone. But that didn't stop her from singing. She sang with more passion and meaning than ever before. When she would sing after she was sick, she would forget the words or fall out of key. But she sang anyway; she worshipped anyway. She didn't care how she sounded or what people thought. She just kept singing, and she never stopped.

One day, my mom was at her worst and bedridden. The only person home with her that morning was her son Matthew. My grandpa came over to say hello to his daughter, and as he opened the front door, he couldn't see anyone but heard music coming from his daughter's bedroom. As he peeked into her room, he found Matthew playing his guitar and singing to his mom, softly and sweetly. Mom, not being able to really speak then, just smiled and tapped her hand to the rhythm. My grandpa was deeply touched by what he saw that day. I would often lay in bed with her and hold her hand and sing praise songs because those were her favorite. Toward the end, that was the only way we could express ourselves to her. Music was a way to feel connected to our mother; it was a way to be close to her. It still is. And no matter how sick she was, her love of music never died. There was not a lot we could do for her; often we felt so powerless and helpless, but we could give her one of the things she loved the most: music.

There was a time we were burdened by silence. There were times where the music stopped. In our hearts, we kept searching for the music. At some point, we started putting pen to paper. We started writing down everything that mattered to us. We wrote down all our fears, joys, and sorrow. These words on paper transformed into lyrics and from there the music flowed. We expressed things we couldn't express with words alone. Sometimes we would write songs on our own, but many times, Matthew and I would come together and write. Matthew and I often felt so burdened and imprisoned, but as that pen glided across the paper, we could feel a release. Singing was one of the only things that helped us feel free.

When my mom passed away, she did not leave us empty-handed. She left us with the gift and love of music. To this day, I sing the same song that she used to sing to me to my kids to help them drift to sleep. And, as I sing to my children, as I hold them in my arms and sing to them the same words my mother sang to me, I feel her with me. I hear her voice, and I hope by singing to them my mother's lullaby they get a glimpse of her. In every tough situation, my mom would do two things: she would pray and she would sing. And that's just what we three kids learned to do when times were rough. If you walked into our house during the time my mother was sick, all you'd hear is music. Whether it was our CD players turned as loud as they could go or the sound of my brother's guitar or just our voices alone. When life was too hard to bear, when pain consumed us, when we had no reason to sing, we sang anyway. Even though things were sad and so very hard in our house, it was always filled with a song. And when we really miss her, we—you guessed it—sing. Because if we sing loud enough and hard enough, we can hear our mother's voice in ours.

Letters of Melody

(Songs written by Maralee Mason and Matthew Nielsen)

To Me You Are Perfect

When I close my eyes I still hear your voice singing me to sleep
And your lips on my cheek as if you were standing there beside me.
I can still see your smile the very smile that changed the world
I can still feel your hand holding mine.
So let's take a walk down by the beach
I'll tell you how my life is going and you can tell me how heaven is.
I will always miss you
I will always love you
I know you will never leave me
And to me you are perfect
So sleep well and I'll see you soon in my dreams
(Written by Matthew Nielsen in 2007)

Can you feel that?

That old table / Where we sat so many times
All the scratches and the edges hold all the years we've cried
And that old house / Where we grew up
So full of chaos but also love
Life wasn't easy / The wind brought more than a breeze
It knocked us to our knees
But can you feel that? Can you feel that?

The warmth on your face / All that time spent in the grey
And the sun finally came

The grass / Where we'd lay on our backs
Starring at blue / Wishing we could move to the moon
And that street / Where we'd laugh and we'd play

And pray that our feet could outrun our fate
The silence could be deadly / But the sound of your guitar carried hope
Can you feel that? Can you feel that?

The warmth on your face / All that time spent in the grey
And the sun finally came

It took so long to get here / So may demons died
All the scars from the battles / Taking back what was mine
Love finally found us right where we stood
It cleared our vision like only love could.
The past is still heavy / There's a weight we still carry
But we no longer carry it alone
Can you feel that? Can you feel that?

The warmth on your face / All that time spent in the grey
And the sun finally came
(Written by Maralee Mason in 2018)

Untitled
Play that song more me again / I've been playing it over in my head
It has all the words I've never said to you
I wish that I could alter time / If only I could press rewind
I would just sit here and listen to you sing
But the clock can't tick backwards / Screaming but life won't stop
And I don't have much of anything / but I'll always have the music

The harmony that takes me away when my heart can't stay
The melody that bring you back when you seem so far away
So far away

Play that guitar for me again / That sound was may sweetest friend
The rhythm how it played to me / When words they failed me
Words they failed me but never in the melody

It's how I reached you / It's how you reached me too

Dejection was everywhere / But our voices filled the air
Never empty handed
You left us with the music / I'll find you in the music

The harmony that takes me away when my heart can't stay
The melody that bring you back when you seem so far away
So far away
(Written by Maralee Mason and Matthew Nielsen in 2015)

Series of Moments
Life is a series of moments / So make the next one count.
The way you live / That moment will determine the outcome of what's yet
to come
Embrace the one you love / Hold tight it's not too long now
I'm sorry I'm sorry I'm selfish
But it's too late you scream you scream
Please don't go I never got to know you
Can I start again? I swear it'll be different,
I'll cry with you laugh with you tell you that I love you
But you're gone
For what it's worth, I'm sorry
Walk away when you know / When she's better than all alone
Show her that you love her / While you still can
You throw away friendships like it's your job / What do you have to prove
Now you're just all alone starving for attention
I'm sorry I'm sorry I'm selfish
But it's too late you scream you scream
Please don't go I never got to know you
Can I start again I swear it will be different
I cry with you laugh with you tell you that I love you but your gone
For what it's worth, I'm sorry.
(Written by Matthew Nielsen in 2007)

61

CHAPTER SIX

The Hum

Some moments are unbelievably beautiful
and I will have never even noticed the hum they make
until those moments have passed.
It's not until I looked back and realize, that's all I get
~ Matthew Nielsen

"You care more about Mom than you do about me!" I bellowed to my dad from the other end of the hall. In return, he hurled a hurtful comment back at me. The hallway was often where we faced our pain. There was so much going on, so many things to process and work through, and as we passed each other in the hall, we would at times work it out on each other. We would just stand in that cursed hallway screaming at each other until our voices grew hoarse. We were all vying for the same woman's love and attention. Although she longed to give that to us, she was not able to. So, we all felt hurt and ignored, alone and afraid. Every day we fought to keep the pain we were feeling inside. But sometimes our life was too much, the pain was too great, and it would become impossible to keep it inside any longer. There were many restless nights when we would cry ourselves to sleep because we felt utterly alone and deeply hurt from the ones we loved the most. Though we could have been each other's solution, we usually just ended up adding to the problem. We could be a great support for each other but also a convenient punching bag. There were times when we drifted far apart, and there were times we let our circumstances come between us. We didn't always agree with our dad's decisions, we didn't always like how someone would handle certain situations, we weren't always on the same page, but we were all we had. Over the years, we tried our hardest to forgive each other. We are still working through the past, through our hurt, and all the things we lost. We still let circumstances get between us. We can often trigger one another. The truth is my mother's sickness broke us, tore us open, and we will forever be marked by it. My mother could be unrecognisable. The cancer changed her. But the truth is the cancer changed all of us. At some point we all became unrecognisable. Life with a sick parent was far from easy. There were many negatives and lots of memories I wish I didn't have—things I often pray I could just forget. My memories are filled with pain, sickness, worry, and regret. Life often seemed more terrible than good. The pain we experienced had so much power and was so complex. It would often bring us together, but sometimes it tore us apart. It bonded us yet isolated us from each other.

Even though life got hard for my family, it was not always that way. There were times where life was good. At times, it even seemed perfect. Underneath all the pain and screams and hurtful words was the strong foundation my parents had built. My parents built our life on something strong—on faith, love and trust. Before and after my mom got sick, my parents did everything they could to make our lives good. My mom loved us kids more than anything. She felt that being our mom was one of the ways she served God. She was super protective and very sweet when life let us down.

The family memories I have are not perfectly recalled, although they feel like they are. Over the years, I have started to realize that I have a filter on some of my memories. That some are based on fantasy not reality. Some of them were just good and some I just need to remember them as good. Here are some of my good family memories as I remember them.

I remember when Matthew and I were little, my parents would take us out on "double dates". My mom and I would wait in our rooms. Matthew would go knock on Mom's door to pick up his "date", and my dad would knock on mine. The boys would often have flowers in hand. I remember waiting for the knock on my door, I was so excited. I remember how it felt when I opened the door to my dad, I felt special and important.

We had pizza and movie nights every Friday without fail. I close my eyes and I can see us in the basement of the house that I grew up in. I can see a cartoon on the TV and the pizza in our hands and the smiles on our faces.

My parents took us on multiple family vacations where we would create memories we could hold on to no matter what came next.

There is one trip in particular that I often play over in my mind. As a family we traveled to Long Beach, BC. I was around twelve or thirteen years old. It was just me, my brother Matthew, my dad, and my mom. We stayed in a small, cheap motel that did not quite meet my mother's high standards, but she pushed to make it work. The hotel had a high price tag for such a small grungy place, but it is what fit my parents' budget at the time. This motel lacked elegance but became the source of our laughter and many jokes.

We spent every day walking along the sandy beaches, dipping our toes in the ocean and exploring this beautiful place. A place that was full of peace and comfort. We breathed in every second not knowing one day we would be lacking in all those things. One day we embarked on a three-hour ocean tour to some natural hot springs; on our way to the springs, we saw all kinds of animals, whales swimming in the ocean and black bears exploring on land. When we reached land, we began an amazing hike through a beautiful green forest. We walked between trees that seemed giant, and we often looked up in awe and wonder. After twenty minutes or so, we reached the hot springs. The springs were not that large; they fit about twenty to thirty people. The warm water was surrounded by rocks and was breathtaking to look at. There was a hot spring located on the ground and one a little higher up. The boys sat in the lower one and my mom and I climbed higher up. We just mostly sat in silence looking out at the most amazing scenery. On that trip, we spent every second together. We ran through the sand with the wind blowing behind us and the waves crashing in front of us. My brother and I chased each other with slimy seaweed we found on the beach, laughing the whole time. The whole vacation was filled with smiles and intense laughter, enjoying each other's company and the time we had. On the last day, we were roaming the beach. Matthew and I were sitting on some giant rocks watching the waves crash against them. As we were enjoying nature, my dad and mom headed up to an abandoned cabin. There my dad took out his small pocketknife and carved a heart with his and my mom's name inside. He wanted to make their mark. He wanted to do something that we would remember forever. He wanted everyone who came across that cabin to know he loved his wife dearly. I dream of one day taking my kids there. Taking them to that old abandoned cabin on the beach and showing them their grandparents' names carved into that old worn wood, showing them the love our family had, telling them stories of that day and making amazing memories of our own. That trip was an amazing adventure, and it is something we have held onto tightly ever since.

I remember when I was around thirteen years old. *Titanic* had just come out in theaters. All my friends had seen it and were bragging about how wonderful and romantic it was, and I begged my parents to let me go. They told me it was too "adult" for me and said I was not allowed to see it. But to me that answer was unacceptable. I felt like I would just die if I didn't see it. So, every day I would beg them to let me go, but the answer was always the same. No. Then one night my mom informed me that we were going to a Bible study at someone's house and that Dad was going to drop us off. So we got in the car and we started to drive to the

Bible study. As we passed the movie theater, I looked up and read the big bright sign that read, "Now Playing: *Titanic*" and my little heart sank. I so badly wanted to be one of those people in that theatre. We then drove through a residential area. My parents started to argue about where the Bible study was. It was apparent to me we were lost. They seemed to be getting angrier and angrier, and I thought sarcastically to myself, "Great, this is exactly how I want to spend my night." My mom looked at my dad and said, "Well, let's just stop and find a phone to get the address!" So, they turned around and my dad started driving by the movie theater once again, but this time, they stopped in front of it and yelled "Surprise! Gotcha!!" They then informed me that my mom and I were going to see *Titanic*! I probably don't have to describe how thrilled I was. Not only did I get to see the movie I had been longing so desperately to see, but I also got an evening out with my mom, just her and me. Of course, she made me go to the bathroom during the more mature parts of the film, but I didn't care. When I look back, it seems so silly that seeing the *Titanic* was so important to me. My mom remembered what it was like to be thirteen and how the strangest things felt like the most important. When I think back on that day, it makes me smile and laugh to think of the great lengths they went to just to surprise me. They loved me so much they were willing to have a fake fight just for me. My parents made it so that throughout my life, no matter what happened, I would have proof of their love for me.

The last family trip we ever took together was to Disneyland. I was fifteen and going through a very tough time because of my mother's illness, but I was so excited to be spending the week with my family and especially my mom. Spending time with my family really put things in perspective for me. It made me appreciate what I had instead of constantly focusing on all the things I was going without.

We stayed in an average hotel with a beautiful pool close to the amusement park. Walking into the park was nothing short of magical. We went on countless rides and ate tons of junk food. We spent many days roaming and exploring all the wonderful things the park had to offer. We experienced so much uninterrupted fun and delight. Partying with Mickey Mouse in the happiest place on earth was a nice break from our normal. One day, we took a break from Disneyland and my parents took us to the beach for the entire day. We swam in the ocean and played in the sand. My mom and I spent part of the afternoon shopping, just her and I, while the boys explored the beach. We tried on lots of clothes, and she bought me the cutest little pink Hawaiian dress. I put it on instantly and wore it for the rest of the day.

My mom was cancer-free at the time but still not feeling one hundred percent. She was always battling something in her body. But no matter how she was feeling physically, she tried to never let it affect our time. She often had a hard time keeping up with us kids, who were always running somewhere, so excited to experience something new. But she did her best. She pushed herself daily, determined to make our vacation great. Disneyland is exhausting for a person in perfect health, so it's pretty impressive how well my mom did, considering all her limitations. She must have been so tired going out almost every day all day, but she never said a word. However, there was one day when she was feeling really sick and she was just too tired to go anywhere. Feeling defeated but still not wanting to spoil our fun, our parents told Matthew and I to go Disneyland on our own, which was huge! My mom was so protective, but she wanted us to have a great time and not be stuck in a hotel all day. So off we went, parent-free with the cellphone in hand and instructions to stick together and call every two hours to check in. She wanted us, if just for a moment, to forget our circumstances and just enjoy the moment and the time we had together. That vacation was like medicine. The fun and laughter gave peace to our hearts and an escape from all that awaited us when we returned.

—

For most of my childhood and teenage years, it was just mom, dad, Matthew, and I. Brian was eleven years older than me and the gap between us took many years to bridge. He moved out when I was ten. He moved thirteen hours away from us, so we only saw him once or twice a year. He started a life of his own complete with a beautiful wife and kids.

There are not many times when we were all together, but there is one day we spent as a family I will never forget. Brian and his family came home for Christmas in 2003. I was eighteen and loved spending time with my niece and nephew. We spent the morning exchanging presents and watching the excitement on Brian's kids' faces as they opened their gifts. We were all together and it felt like we had never been apart. Later that night, my brothers dragged a mattress out into the living room. The kids were lying on it and the rest of us were lounging on the couches talking and drinking hot beverages by the lights of the Christmas tree. Then, suddenly, the lights went out and it was pitch black. My dad got some flashlights and candles. Soon the room was lit by beautiful candlelight. Matthew grabbed his guitar and started to play for us. Soon my brothers and I were singing songs for our parents.

My parents sat there and just listened to their children sing together. They looked so proud, and as my mom let the music wash over her, she looked so peaceful and happy. The power stayed out for hours, and we enjoyed every minute of it. When the power came back on that night, we felt so disappointed. We were having such a good time, and we did not want it to end, so Dad shut off the lights, and we continued to talk and sing.

—

My parents worked so hard building a strong foundation filled with good memories so that when the hard times came rolling in, we had something good to hold onto. When it felt like we were drowning in our grief, we had something to keep us afloat. They may not have always done or said the right thing, and sometimes they really hurt us, but I know they did the best they could in a terrible situation. At times, for me, their best did not always seem good enough. But it did teach me that through everything, in the midst of hard times and tragedy, it is important to remember the good that has been given to you and to hold on to the good things in life and to never let go.

In the beginning of my mom's illness, she was away a lot of the time, so my dad took on both parenting roles. Even though he, frankly, made a terrible mother, he made up for it by being a wonderful dad. With our mom unable to do a lot of things, he took responsibility for cooking the meals. We always joked that his dinners were like eating roadkill. The food was definitely not like mom used to make—that was for sure. But with time he improved greatly. He learned to cook, or at least not poison his children. He cleaned and did the laundry, he picked up all my mom's slack, and he did it happily. And on top of all that, he worked really hard at his job so we would have food, clothes, and shelter. He really did try to be everything we needed, although he couldn't always be everything. He quickly became someone we could depend on. My brothers and I could bring anything to him, and he would try his best to listen to our every word no matter what we had to tell him. My brothers and I asked his advice on relationships, love, anything and everything. There was nothing we couldn't tell him.

I am sure he wanted to scream and plug his ears when we revealed certain things to him. But he never did. He never got mad at us for our mistakes; he just helped us work through them. He made sure we always had someone to hear what we had to say. It got harder for him to be what we needed as we got older and my mom got sicker. It became a struggle balancing kids and a sick wife. But he never stopped trying and giving his best to his family and that showed.

The sicker my mom got, the lonelier she became. Friends didn't come around nearly as often anymore. All she had was her family. So, we strived to become the best friends she ever had. We wanted to be what she desperately needed. Most nights were spent at my parents' house during the last couple years of my mother's life. We did many things together. I told my mom all about my day. I painted her nails, did her hair, and we often had girly movie nights. Dad took her on dates regularly, and Matthew watched TV with her, took her for walks, and played music for her.

Almost a year before she died, she was admitted to the hospital. And for two straight days, she wanted to be holding one of her family member's hands at all times. She couldn't express it with words, but if we were sitting by her bedside and holding her hand and tried to get up, she wouldn't let us go. The only way one person could get up was if another one would quickly take their place. So, for days we took turns holding her hand. She wanted us close to her. I think just having our hands in hers gave her comfort.

We were the only people in the world who knew how we were feeling, who knew our pain and what it was like at home, what it was like to watch someone you love so much drift away from you.

Sometimes I find myself drowning in regret. Wishing I paid more attention to those moments. I regret not truly living in those moments and not soaking up every minute of them while they were happening. I focused too much on the pain, the sickness, the disappointment and on what my family was getting wrong. I put too much energy into the fights and the grudges and all the things I was losing and not enough into the beauty that surrounded me and the things that were right in front of me. I was more present in the sorrow then I was in the joy. I try to gather all the pieces of memories and try my best to put them together like puzzle. I wish

I memorized the way those happy moments felt and the sound they made. I never noticed before that happiness and beauty made a noise. My brother calls it a hum. This subtle noise that was so quiet you didn't even know it was there. So subtle that we often missed it. I wish I took note of my mom's smile and her grace. The way she looked before she was sick, the sound of her voice, the comfort of her touch. I paid more attention to the lows than I did the highs. I memorized details of the rough times, the sickness, my mom's face when she had a seizure, the way her hand felt when she died. I wish I remembered the good in as much detail as I remember the bad. I should have locked those beautiful things away in my heart, I should have studied them instead of taking those things for granted, because I didn't know their value until they were gone, until she was gone. I wish I memorized every detail of the laughter and the joy. I wish I committed it to memory, I wish I knew it by heart. I wish I was more present, and more intentional, and that I would have savored each moment, instead of just letting them pass me by. I feel like I sometimes squandered the gifts and moments that were given to me, but I didn't know that was all I was going to get, I thought that there would be more. I thought I had more time. If I would have known, I would have treated those moment as precious as they were. I would have taken my time in each one instead of rushing through. But I can't go back, but I can take notice now. I will pay attention to the beauty around me, I will memorize the way it makes me feel and the sound it makes. I will take the time to hide away the precious moments in my mind. I can't and I won't waste what I've been given.

Letters of Love and Devotion

(Journal entries written by Kathleen)

Dear Jesus,
Show us concerning Maralee's education. Speak to us about what we should do. Cover her every day she is at school. Keep her safe. Grant her favor among her classmates.

Thank you for making Maralee a very happy girl. Lord, I praise You for her wonderful attitude, continue to soften her heart towards others; let her giving attitude be a testimony to others. I pray that you would continue to give Chris and me wisdom on raising her and developing her strengths and the direction You want her to go in her life. Amen

Lord,
Thank You, Lord, for Brian's salvation; for the plans that You have for his life, thank You for the occupation You have for him and praise You, Jesus for the Godly woman You have set apart for him. Prepare him for his adult life, Lord, don't let him miss what You have for him. Speak to him, continually show him that You are with him moment by moment, leading and guiding him.

Thank you for my family, for Chris, continue to help him be the head of the home and help me to relinquish all that You want me to make our marriage a happy one. Help us to put one another first in our relationship. I pray for Maralee and Matthew, that You would develop those gifts and talents that You have given them and help us to recognize and develop them. Amen.

Lord,
Thank You for watching over me and always being here, help me not to neglect You. Prepare me for the things to come. I pray for this to come. I

pray for this Thursday at the Christian Ladies meeting that You give me boldness and strength and that You would bless those who hear. Heal my relationship with Chris. Change Brian's heart and make him a responsible adult. Bless Maralee in school and give her good relationships with the teachers and students; find her a good Christian friend. Help me with Matt at home so I can deposit good things into him. I thank You for everything in my life; there are so many things to pray for, just help me to get through them all, in Jesus' name, Amen.

Heavenly Father,
I pray for our children. That You would lead, guide, and protect them in all they do. Cause Brian to mature, able to stand on his own two feet. Be with Maralee at school, grant her favor among the teachers and students, give her mind clarity of thought, speak to her and help her to hear your voice.

I rebuke that lying spirit, you stay away from her, I bind you! Thank you for giving Matt an interest in the things of God. Help us to guide and direct him in all the areas of his life.

To Maralee,
As your mother and your father
We are very proud of you
If you ask don't bother
We love you
As we love your brother Matthew
The things you have done in life
Have been immeasurable above all measure
Maralee you are our big treasure
We will love you forever.
Love, Mom
(A letter written before my mom was sick)

Even So

To Mom,

I love you and I miss you. How are you feeling? I am praying for you. How is it going? Say hi to Dad and tell him I love him.

All my love,

Matthew

(age 7, written while my mom was in Vancouver for treatment)

To Mom,

I love you and miss you so much. When you get home, I'll make you supper. I will be praying for you every day and night. Tell Dad that I love him and miss him a lot. I beat Grandpa and Grandpa and Aunty Becky at Skip Bo. Don't forget to phone me and Matthew. If you can, phone in the morning and at night. I love you Mom with all my heart.

All my love,

Maralee

P.S. Get Well Soon

(written while my mom was in Vancouver for treatment)

To Mommy,

You are beautiful and I love you. No matter what happens, you will always be my mom. I want to have a heart like yours. I pray that a part of you lives in me. I long to be like you.

Have a good day, Mommy!

Love,

Maralee

(a letter written in 2002)

CHAPTER SEVEN

Fighting for You

And I'll rise up high like the waves
I'll rise up in spite of the ache
I'll rise up and I'll do it a thousand times again
For you
~ Andra Day

Every day it seemed we were losing our mother more and more. We witnessed her slipping further and further away from us. She was always right in front of us, so close we could reach out and touch her, but at the same time, she was so far away. We tried not to treat her any differently, but that was hard to do because she was so different. How do you treat someone like a mother when you are the one taking care of them? How do you speak to someone like an adult when they act like a child? It was hard trying to find the balance in how we spoke and acted toward her. Her mind may have been drifting, but she understood things. She was smarter than people gave her credit for. There were friends of hers who would speak to her like she was a baby every time they would visit, and you could tell by the look on her face she hated it. We didn't want to disrespect her in any way, so we tried to treat her the same as we always had.

There were times when she was not the only one drifting away.

We all started to grow weary and tired. We pulled away from each other and from God. We seemed to slowly be losing ourselves, but in spite of that, we tried desperately to hold on. But with every breath she missed, with every pain, every time she drifted a little further away, so did we. Her pain was our pain. When she suffered, so did we. It was torture to watch our mother slip away and become a woman we did not recognize. While witnessing her suffering, we became unable to recognize ourselves.

In 2005, Kathleen slowly started to lose the ability to speak. Expressing herself to us became harder and harder. We never really knew what she was feeling or what she wanted, and her frustration was written all over her face. It was similar to an infant or toddler before they learn to speak. There was a lot of guessing and charades to figure out what she needed or wanted.

One night, when I was about twenty years old, I came over to my parents' house with a migraine. It was really bad, so I laid my head down on my mom's lap and said, "Mommy, my head hurts." She took her hand and rubbed my head. As she rubbed my head and brushed my hair with her fingers, tears poured down my face. They were not tears of sadness; I was just so touched that no matter what kind of state she was in, she never stopped being my mom. When I was pregnant with my first baby, she would always lift up my shirt so she could kiss and rub my belly. Every time she did, it completely warmed my heart. You could always see her trying her absolute hardest to do whatever she could to be there for us. She may not have been able to perform motherly duties anymore, but she was the greatest mom because she always gave us all she had—even if it was just her putting her hand in mine after I'd had a bad day. Or her placing her hand on my cheek so I knew she loved me.

I once read something that asked a great question. It said something like, "Say one person gave someone in need twenty dollars and another person gave only five, but then you found out that the first person had a million dollars and the second only had five. Who gave more?" My mom did not have a lot to give, but she held nothing back. She kept nothing to herself. She kept trying to be our mother until she simply no longer could. Every effort she made may have seemed small to anyone else, but to me, everything she did, no matter how small the gesture, felt huge. She kept on giving of herself even on her deathbed. Being a mother it something she always wanted. it was something she had fought so hard for, and she was not going to give that up. I couldn't ask for a better mom than one who keeps on giving even when she has little to give.

It was six days into 2007, when I got a call late at night from my dad. He informed me that my mom was not doing so well and that he had called 911. An ambulance came to the house and rushed her to the hospital. By the time the ambulance got her to the hospital, she was barely breathing and had slipped into a coma. We walked through the hospital doors and approached the front desk, and the receptionist told us that my mom had been admitted to the ICU. We walked into the ICU, and our hearts suddenly sank when we saw her unconscious and hooked up to all kinds of machines and tubes. We hated seeing her like that. When we arrived, it was late at night, so my dad, Matthew, my husband, and I spent the night in the waiting room, sleeping in small uncomfortable chairs. We did not want to leave her side. The next evening, after a long and tiring day of sitting by my mom's bedside, the doctor called us into a meeting room. The oncologist sat us down and told us they performed a CAT scan and discovered there were tumors in my mom's brain. We just sat there in that cold, beige meeting room, staring at the floor trying to absorb the news. We tried so hard to fight the tears, but we quickly lost that fight. After years of being in remission from the cancer, it was back. As if things weren't bad enough, cancer had to weasel its way back into our life. I don't think we loathed anything as much as we did that ruthless disease. And before the shock wore off from the news, the doctor coldly told us that our mom would not make it through the week, and there was absolutely no chance we could take her home.

My dad looked the doctor straight in the eyes as if he hadn't heard a word of what the doctor had just told us and said, "I will bring her home."

The doctor rudely replied, "No you won't."

"I have hope," my dad said. "I will bring her home."

The doctor rolled his eyes and left the room annoyed.

Mom was admitted into the family room, a room we hated and dreaded. It is the room they put you in when they are sure the patient will not make it. Almost every time my mom was admitted to the hospital, she was placed in this room. Things were looking grim, so I called my brother Brian to let him know about the situation. I took the elevator to the hospital lobby, walked down a long narrow hallway, and sat down in an old raggedy chair that sat in front of a pay phone. With a very heavy heart, I dialed his number.

"Hello?" Brian answered.

"Hi," I said with sadness in my voice.

Right away, Brian knew that something was wrong. "What is it?" he asked.

I took a big breath in, and as I let it out, I answered, "Mom is in the hospital. The cancer is back."

Brian sighed, "How is she?"

Tears were streaming down my cheeks. "Not well. They say she won't make it. I think you should come home."

Two days later, Brian was home. As a family, we waited, cried, prayed and hoped.

Weeks of agonizing waiting went by and just when we thought for a moment that this could really be the end, she opened her eyes. And after some time of recovery, my dad did just what he said he would do—he brought her home.

～

After waking from the coma, my mom's decline accelerated.

After coming home, she never walked again. She used a wheelchair, relying on her family to take her where she needed or wanted to go. Slowly her body just started to give up. She soon lost the movement in her right arm. She had a tube placed in her stomach because she lost the ability to properly chew and swallow her food, and her lungs were collecting too much fluid. At this point, she was completely dependent on us to take care of her. You could tell by looking into her eyes that it pained her to be so dependent on her family.

Her mind might have been slipping away, but she was aware enough to know what was happening to her, and you could tell that she hated it. It often seemed like she was a prisoner in her own body. But she had no choice; the basic daily routines were now impossible to do. The hardest part for us to witness was the loss of her visible joyful spirit.

My mom's fight against cancer was a long and tiring one. She fought with all her might for twelve years. She faced hundreds of doctor visits, a thousand seizures, at least eight hospital admittances and four comas.

After each coma, the doctors told us she would never wake up and death was coming. As a family, we tried to be as strong as my mother was, but we often failed. We tried to show the same faith she did. We tried with everything we had to hold on to her and ourselves. But the question that constantly played in our minds, the question we couldn't shake was, "How do I hold onto something? How do I fight for something I feel like I have already lost?" Our mother was physically with us, but the woman and mother we remembered and missed was no longer there. Our greatest fear was that she was not coming back. We were told so many times that she wasn't going to make it, and almost every time, she did. We would face devastating news, so we would say our goodbyes and prepare ourselves for the worst. And although we were thrilled when she recovered—because losing her in any respect was the worst thing to imagine—the whole ordeal was almost as terrible, it was a little like having her pass and then come back to life and then pass and then come back to life. It was a roller coaster, one we could not get off, one with so many ups and downs and twists and turns it made us sick. But we kept on with the terrible because it was better than the alternative, which was not getting her back at all. My mother was strong and she was brave, but she was reaching a point where she could not do much fighting, we were proudly fighting alongside her, but now we had to start fighting for her. We needed to rise—hoping, even when the well seemed dry. We kept on fighting for our mother, being the voice she didn't have, being her strength, executing the faith she couldn't always show. So, when the doctors told us the news we always dreaded, that same speech we heard far too often, those exact words that broke our hearts every single time, we stood strong, as strong as we could, not for us but for her. That news had never been acceptable to our mother, so it was not acceptable to us. Each time we fought on her behalf, each time we stood when we barely had the strength to, the ache got more intense. But no matter the pain we rose anyway. Each time adding more weight to our burdened hearts. We were worn and tired, but we didn't stop.

My father was the one who did all of this absolutely beautifully. The warrior he transformed into for the sake of his wife was nothing short of inspiring. Every time we got the dreaded news, my dad would look the doctor straight in the eye and say, "God will heal her. I have faith. And I will bring her home." And each time that is just what he did.

CHAPTER EIGHT

The Side Effects of Sorrow

Standing on the edge looking over
Then that dark night got a little colder
I was chased there by my demons, the only thing I still believed in
~Maralee Mason

Four years into my mother's sickness, depression swept through our home like wildfire. Sadness seemed to swallow us whole, and we were too weak to fight against it. At age fifteen, I became its victim. One night, my mom burst into my room and started yelling at me, for no real reason at all. I just sat there on my bed, staring out the window as she screamed at me, wishing I could be anywhere but there. When she got like that, which was often around that time in her sickness, I would usually just sit and take it, but this time, I couldn't. I couldn't take it for a moment longer. And all of a sudden in the middle of her screaming at me, I thought, "That's it!" I jumped from my bed and I ran past my mom to the bathroom, opened the cupboard, and grabbed a bottle of pills, my parents' cellphone, and ran out the door, slamming it behind me. I started thinking to myself, "I can't do this anymore! Life shouldn't be this hard." I remember thinking, "It hurts too badly, it just hurts too much, and I can't feel this way any longer." I had the responsibilities of an adult, and I was expected to act like one, but I didn't know how because I wasn't one. I was just a kid. The pressure of that on top of all the normal teenage girl things I had to face—like friends, boys, and self-esteem—all while not being able to talk to my mom about it got to be too much. I just lost it. For years, every pain, ever tear, every disappointment had piled up, and it finally gave way.

I ran as fast as my legs would allow to a park down the street from my house. When I got to the gate, I stopped, and then I walked slowly into the park. I sat on the cold wet grass in the middle of the field and stared at the bottle of pills. I fought with myself for a while. I didn't really want to die, but I also didn't want to feel that way anymore.

For some reason I am still somewhat unaware of, I was also mad at myself, and I thought I needed to be punished. Maybe I thought I should have been handling things better or been a better caregiver for my mom, who knows. I just wanted the pain to stop, and perhaps I just wanted to know if my mom still loved me. Maybe I just wanted to see if anybody loved me, for I was hardly ever the focus. I called a friend, hoping they could help, maybe even talk me out of it. But it didn't help; for some reason, I felt worse. I hung up the phone abruptly and took the entire bottle of pills. My body was no longer my own. I no longer had control. I had given in to sadness.

I laid on my back and cried. I felt so scared and alone, not just in the park that night but always. I started to realize what I had just done, and in the moment, I knew I didn't really want my life to end. Panic consumed me and I ran to a family friend's house, too scared to go home and face my parents. I stood on their front step sobbing, when I rang the doorbell, I felt my stomach sink. They opened it to me and brought me inside. I promptly confessed what I had done and then they quickly called my parents. My dad showed up moments later; he was so mad, he wouldn't even look at me. As we drove down my street toward our home, I saw a police car in our driveway. The friend I had called earlier had phoned the police. I cannot imagine how scared my parents were when the doorbell rang and they opened to an officer asking them if they knew where I was. Their hearts must have stopped. My dad left the car slamming the door behind him and my mom got in the driver's seat. I suppose my dad was just too furious and distraught to take me. By then, whatever made her so angry before had left and she was herself again. It often worked that way—one minute my mom would be one person and the next someone completely different. She could change within a matter of seconds; she would go from comfort to terror in mere moments. As she sat in the seat beside me, she seemed very upset and worried. The car ride to the hospital seemed so long; the only sound was my crying. Hand in hand, my mother and I walked through the hospital doors. She told me to wait while she found someone to help me, when she returned she found me on my knees crying so uncontrollably, crying so intensely it barley gave me time to breathe, which was all right with me cause with every breath I took in more pain came with it. A nurse and my mom picked me up off the floor and walked me into the emergency room. I was admitted in the ICU overnight.

I was forced to drink the vilest liquid. A terrible charcoal drink that would help dissolve the pills I took. I could barely sleep that night in that hospital room; humiliation and sadness overwhelmed me. The next morning, my dad walked into my room and sat by my bedside. He didn't look mad anymore, just sad and hurt. I felt terrible. He had been hurt enough, and I had just made it worse.

With tears in his eyes, he told me he loved me and that he didn't want to lose me. He apologized for getting mad; he said he just did not know how to cope with it. He held me close and then handed me a small box. As he handed it to me, he told me it was supposed to be for my sixteenth birthday, but he wanted me to have it now. I slowly opened it. It was a ring, gold with four little hearts. "It was your mother's engagement ring," my dad said with a smile.

"Thank you," I said softly, almost too emotional to speak. The love my father showed me that day was just what I needed.

I cried for the next couple of days. Feelings of shame,

embarrassment, pain, and sadness overcame me. I could not believe what I had done or understand the choices I made that day. I was so afraid that I would not be able to handle what came next. My mom was getting sicker and my dad sadder. Life was weighing down on me, and I just didn't think I was strong enough to carry the weight. I was losing myself.

For years, I was not the woman I wanted to be. With every passing year, the sorrow I felt became greater and the burden heavier. I tried so hard to fight against it, but I lost every time. It got so bad that I felt like nothing but a shell. I tried to be hopeful, but I knew things at home weren't going to get better, and maybe neither would I.

———

Anger was one of the many major side effects of brain cancer but knowing that didn't make it any easier to deal with. My mother's mood swings happened often and they had great power behind them. While she would be getting mad at me for no reason at all, I would try to tell myself, "It's not her fault, she's sick," but it didn't make her words any less painful. As I got older, her mood swings got worse. When I was eighteen, I couldn't even be in a room with her without her yelling at me. She would tell me she hated me and call me names. Once she was so mad, she even pulled a knife on me. She held the knife up in front of her chest and chased me around the kitchen table with it. "It's not her fault. She's sick. It's not her fault. She's sick," I would tell myself over and over.

I had to remind myself daily that the person in front of me wasn't who my mother really was. Although that gave me some comfort, her anger still took a toll on me, and it often messed with my mind. I started to believe the lies that entered my head that my mother didn't love me anymore and maybe she really meant the things she was saying. There was a period of about three years where she hardly ever spoke to me calmly. I knew the anger was just a stage and that it would end, but even when it did, and she moved on to the childlike stage, all the things she said and did toward me never left. I carried them with me for many years.

I suffered greatly from depression well into my twenties. Suicide was a constant thought in my head. I spent countless nights locked in the bathroom, hiding. I just sat on the cold tile floor staring at bathroom cleaners trying to fight the urge to drink them. I have had many panic attacks over the last twenty years. I don't always see them coming. They sneak up on me. I can go from coping to full panic in mere moments. Everything goes blurry. Nothing is in focus. My breath quickens, at times I can't catch it at all. I try and control it, but it overtakes me. My heart races and hurts, my arms start to tingle, and then go numb as I clench my chest and I sincerely wonder if the pain will kill me. All I can see is red and I am always shocked by the amount of tears that stream from my eyes. My entire body hunches forwards and I become frozen. I cannot move. I'm trapped. Usually words come easy to me, but in these moments, I can't find them, and if I do, I often regret them. I struggle to fight against the panic that consumes me, but in that moment, control is no longer mine. My mind leaves the present and transports me into a different moment. A moment of the past. I question what brought me back. Was it the words someone said to me in passing? Was it a look from a loved one? Was it fight? A song? A movie? A smell? In an instant, I go from living in the moment to reliving the past. I feel the same as if I was experiencing the trauma all over again. It is terrifying. I can see my mother's face as if she was right in front of me. I relive my pain and hers. I see the little girl I used to be, and I relive her pain too. I try to bring myself back to reality, but I can't get a firm grip on what is real and what is the past. It all seems to blend into a bury haze.

My erratic behavior pushed everyone I loved away. No one could understand why I was acting the way I was. No one could believe I had no control when I had attacks. I was often surrounded by people, by friends, but I really felt all alone. Almost every choice I made was driven by my sadness and my desperate need for love.

I often walked around feeling like I was not loved enough. It did not take long for depression to be what I was known for. I was "the sad one," "the messed up one." Everyone knew about the sadness I felt. I couldn't hide it. It consumed me; it became who I was. I never felt happy. There were times when I would smile and laugh, but no matter what was happening on the outside, on the inside I was in pain—heart-wrenching agony. One night, I was once again close to suicide. I felt like I was losing everything. Things that would make anyone sad would simply devastate me. I couldn't take any disappointment or hurt. I was already filled with pain from dealing with my mom's sickness, and I felt so rejected at home because my parents didn't have time to truly embrace me. I couldn't take any more pain, any more disappointment, or any more rejection. I had my fill. I just needed something else, something good. It was late one night past midnight, I was driving, and it took all I had not to drive off the road. I just wanted it all to end.

I eventually parked the car and got out a pocketknife that was kept in the glove compartment, and I started to cut my arms. Fear overtook me and I called a friend. She came and hugged me and listened to me. She tried to convince me to go to the hospital. She knew I needed help, but I would not go. I couldn't. She drove me home, and as soon as I arrived, I ran into the bathroom and hid. My friend came in and told my dad what had happened. I just stayed in the bathroom ashamed and embarrassed. I eventually came out and my friend and dad sat up with me and talked with me until I was ready to go to sleep.

The very next night, there was a young adults Christmas party at my church. There was square dancing. I danced, smiled, laughed and do-si-doed. I appeared to be having a great time. About a week later, a friend said to me that it bugged him that I would be so sad one night and then happy the next. I guess it was hard to believe I was really sad if I could turn it on and off like that. I paused for a moment, then responded, "If I don't laugh and smile, I will fall apart." In order for me to make it, I had to fake it. And sometimes I did it well and sometimes not so much.

But one day, I had enough. I was done with being ruled by my sadness and my circumstances.

It happened during a Bible study. I started to feel really bad. I could feel myself start to panic. I ran out of the building and all the way home. I felt so crazy and sad. I was shaking and crying and feeling like I was going to be sick. My brother, scared and worried for me, ran back to the Bible study and got a friend of mine and the woman leading the Bible study and brought them back home (he didn't want to wake my dad). They stayed with me for hours that night. They held me and prayed with me. I cried to the point where there wasn't room for breath. I cried out to God with all of my heart. In that moment, something switched, something changed. The heaviness of my heart was lifting. I started laughing. I started to feel hopeful, like maybe things could be better. Then I got a glimpse of a feeling that was so foreign to me, happiness. It had been a while since I had felt that emotion. I can't explain what happened that night, how one moment I was gripped with sadness, and the next I was reaching for happiness. It sounds so strange, and it was. I suppose I just hit a wall and I could let it stop me and or I could climb over. Perhaps after years of faking it and reciting affirmations I really didn't believe, my brain had finally start to accept it and receive it as the truth. No matter what caused the shift inside me, I am grateful. Had I lived any longer consumed with that sadness, I truly believe I would have died.

After that night, I started clean, but my new start wasn't quick or easy. I became a fighter. I started to fight for the day where I would no longer let my fears and sadness rule me. After that night, happiness was no longer a stranger, but I could never fully shake the sadness. I couldn't fully shake certain memories from my mind. Daily, my past would catch up to me. I was haunted by my sorrow well into my marriage. Even after someone chose me, loved me, and saw me; even after I got what I desired, what my heart had been craving for so long, I still struggled. I struggled with the fear of being rejected by the one I loved the most, the fear that one day I wouldn't be loved by him anymore. Anytime I didn't feel loved (justified or not) I would panic, just like I did when I was a teenager. I would wrestle with my breath, and my body would be filled with physical pain. I was fed up with being a prisoner of my past, and I was concerned for my marriage, so I made a choice to get some help. I started seeing a counselor who referred me to a psychologist. After explaining my symptoms to them each separately, they both had come to the same conclusion. That conclusion was that I was most likely suffering from post-traumatic stress disorder (PTSD). Circumstances in my life would trigger a feeling or a memory inside of me and I would be transported back to when I was a kid. This disorder made me easily spooked, overwhelmed, and extremely more sensitive than I already was. After hearing this, everything made so much more sense. I had realized that I had been suffering from this for many years. After I realized this, after I realized I had something real, that I wasn't weak, that I wasn't a terrible person, I felt free. It reminded me of the story of when my mom found out she had cancer. She was relieved. She was glad there was a reason behind all the changes she couldn't control, changes she blamed herself for. I worked even harder after that. After James (my husband) and I knew what was happening, we were able to change things. And now, I am finally truly moving forward. My panic attacks are getting further and further apart. And finally, I am at the point where the happy outweighs the sad.

I have dark days still. I am human. I get sad. I cry. I cry a lot. I will always cry over what I lost. Some days, panic attacks creep back in. A circumstance, a song, a picture can still transport me back in time. My mind still gets triggered, and for a moment I feel trapped in the past. But what is different is that I use all my might to make sure I don't stay in that place. I've already spent too much time there. I have also learned there is healing in the pain. So, when it comes, I embrace it. I feel it and then I keep moving forward. I will never stop moving forward and I will never let depression, pain, sadness, or circumstance rule me again.

⸺

My brother Matthew also faced depression throughout his teen years, but he dealt with his sadness in a different way. I indulged in my sadness and he indulged in things to distract him from his. He too felt like he wasn't loved enough, so he went searching for what he desperately longed for. But no matter what he did, he could not escape the truth. His mother was sick, his father was falling apart with grief, and his sister was being suffocated by depression. His family was drifting away.

One Christmas Eve, my family and I were upstairs and Matthew and Mom had a fight. It ended with her slapping him across the face. Not hard enough to physically hurt, but emotionally, he felt destroyed. He immediately ran downstairs into his bedroom and slammed the door. I ran after him. I opened his door and slowly walked in closing the door behind me. He was sitting on his floor with his face in his hands, crying. I sat next to him and put my arm around my brother's shoulders, knowing how he felt, because it had happened to me many times. Matthew looked up at me and said, "The hardest part is that, I honestly don't know if she loves me anymore."

"I know," I said with tears streaming down.

Our dad entered the room, with sadness across his face. He pleaded with us not to be mad at her; he told us that she didn't know what she was doing and that she wasn't herself. We told him that we knew that, but the truth didn't make it hurt any less.

When Matthew was twelve, I noticed how sad he was becoming. His sadness often went unnoticed by our parents who had their own sadness and struggles to attend to, which were all-consuming. He was a lot better at hiding it than I was. But sometimes, when I would be sitting in the living room, I could hear crying coming from his room. He was such a private person. He would try to hide his pain, but I knew. I could see it. He was a boy whose heart was deeply burdened, and he didn't know how to make it go away. A kid is supposed to have parents to run to, but Matthew never felt like he could. He had his parents in body, but in spirit, he felt alone. He had no escape and no release.

The older Matthew got, the harder it became. He made his life busy and filled it with friends in an attempt to be happier. But none of that worked too well for him. Nothing seemed to fill the void he felt. But one day, he started to share in our mother's love for music. He found her old guitar and taught himself how to play. He started writing his feelings down and expressing them through song. The emotion in his songs was beautiful. When we would hear him sing, we would be surprised by the lyrics in his songs; we usually wouldn't know what was hurting him until we heard him sing about it. After so many years, he finally found a way to free himself. He found something to turn to. He started doing what our mother taught him—and that was to sing. When things were hard, he sang. When he wanted to give up, he sang. When sadness was all around, he sang. When he didn't feel like it, he sang. And by doing that, he felt closer to her, and that made all the difference.

My dad watched his kids struggle with their mother's sickness and it pained him greatly. When Matthew entered his teen years, it got harder for my dad to think about us because his entire focus was on his wife. All his thoughts were wrapped up in the fear that he might lose her. The more he thought about that fear, the sadder he became. He could not bear even the thought of living without his wife. He no longer had a partner in life and that truth destroyed him. The loneliness crushed him. Every word he spoke was from a place of sadness. When we would discuss the possibility of losing Mom, he would say, "When she goes, I want to go," and he really meant it. He would often talk about putting a bullet in his head, just so he could escape life. Those words were painful for us to hear. We were already losing our mother, and now we were scared we would lose our father too. I remember finding a bottle of pills in his drawer and I started seeing him take them when he didn't really need them. I told the doctor about the pills and my fear that my dad would take his own life. The doctor advised me to flush the pills and that is what I did. Dad was so angry with me. He "needed" those pills because they numbed him. And he wanted to be numb because if he felt all of his pain, he was scared he would end it all. He never attempted suicide, but it was a constant thought on his mind. By the end, my dad was wrecked and beat by his grief.

Depression had such a strong grip on him, he would walk around for weeks barely saying a word. He often had great bursts of anger, and it would be directed at whomever was in the room at the time. He reached a point where he was so full of pain, it was always overflowing, and he could not control it. It just seeped out of him. There was not enough room inside his soul to store it. Grief and pain ware painted across his face. He couldn't hide it, and he didn't care to try. He got to a point where he'd barely smile or laugh, and when he did smile, it was while he was looking at my mother. Since she was the only one, the only thing that could make him smile, he was scared that if she died, he would be nothing and would have nothing. She was his light—at times, his only light. Without her, he was scared there would be nothing but darkness.

For years, he lived feeling empty and sad. Under all that sadness, fear, depression, and suicidal thoughts was hope, peace, grace, comfort, strength, and love. And I think that is what saved him. And after many years, he would find the light once again.

My mother also faced sadness. In the beginning of her illness, when she was at the cancer clinic by herself, she often felt alone and scared. And some days, sorrow overtook her. It was hard to feel happy when she felt so sick every single day. She was such a strong woman. She had faith and hope like no other, but she was still human, and the world sometimes got to her.

As time went on, it became harder to tell what was really going on inside her head, but other times, it was obvious. Sometimes when I had to change her, she would lay completely still; she wouldn't look me in the eye. She would just stare blankly at the wall, and you knew she was trying to imagine herself somewhere else. There were days when she wouldn't even move, and she would look so sad and heartbroken. There were many times when she would just break down and cry. I never really knew the exact reasons she would get so upset because she could not express them to me. For years, she was so joyful, but after time, the sickness robbed her. But no matter how sad and defeated my mom felt, when you looked deep into her eyes, you could see joy and light—even though she couldn't always feel it or see it. It was there because true joy can never be taken from you.

—

To this day, we struggle with losing our mother and my dad struggles with the loss of his wife. We grieve daily for what we never had and what we will miss out on. And for Matthew and me, we've lived the majority of our lives without a mother. We both feel the absence of our mom every day. There are nights when we just sob, for no reason other than that we miss our mom. The things we had to deal with growing up sometimes haunt us and burden our hearts. I often find myself in amazement that we made it through and that we are still standing. Because of the foundation our lives were built on, because we stayed planted on that foundation, no amount of rain could wash it away.

Though you have made me see troubles, many and bitter, you will restore my life again; from the depths of the earth you will again bring me up. You will increase my honor and comfort me once more. Psalms 71:2-21 (NIV)

Letters from a Grieving Daughter

(Entries found in my journals, written between
the ages of sixteen and eighteen)

I do not feel like I have a mother anymore, even though my mother is very much alive. She'll never be like she once was. Even though I physically have a mom, emotionally I do not. I love her with all my heart don't get me wrong. I just wish I had someone to talk to about guys, love, or life in general. I envy all my friends for they have what I do not.

Mom,
You are currently upstairs sleeping. Even though your body is in your bed and in your clothes, you're not really truly here. I miss you, Mommy. I need you more than I could have ever imagined. My heart breaks from your sickness and my very being aches for your love. You say you love me. Do you truly know that I love you with my whole heart? I wish things were different. I wish you didn't leave me, and I still hope you'll come back. I love you and miss you.
Love,
Maralee

Dear God,
Lord, I lift my family to You. I want freedom in my family and healing and happiness. Change them. God, help them grow. Fill them with peace and Your love and comfort. Thank You.

Dear God,
I pray for the issue with my mom. It's hurting me very badly. Please heal her or help me cope with it. Help me be patient and understanding. But thank You for the fact that she's alive. Thanks for my dad and brother;

they're awesome. I don't know what I'd do without them. Help them in whatever area they need help in and keep them safe and healthy.

Dear God,
I'm feeling very sad, and at times it feels like You're not with me and I wonder where You are. But deep inside my heart, I know You are with me. This pain I'm feeling is starting to overwhelm me, and I feel like I am going to explode. I'm trapped. At times it feels like I can't breathe. I'm suffocating. God help me catch my breath. I need to breathe again. I need to be happy again, truly happy. I need You; please help me. I'm starting to let go. I'm slipping. I'm dying inside. I'm starting to let go. Don't let me slip. Don't let me die. I am so mad and full of anger. At times I feel like I'm mad at You, even though I know I shouldn't be. But why is this happening to me? Why am I so sad? Why is my mom so sick? Why is my family falling apart? Why?! What did we do to deserve this? What did I do? I don't want to be mad at You, and I am sorry that I am. Please forgive me. Please forgive the mistakes I've made and still am making. I want to be close to You. I want to please you in all I do. Just please don't leave me. Please unload all this pain. I hurt so very badly. My heart is broken; can You put it back together again?

Dear God,
I lift up my family. Keep them safe and healthy. Help them through these tough times. Thank You for my family; they're wonderful. I love them so much. I cast out any sadness, depression, anger out of my family in Your name. Thank You for the changes You're going to make in my family and my life.

Dear God,
I feel so good! So happy. I don't think I have ever felt so happy. Thank You for filling me with joy. Today I didn't cry. I haven't cried in so long. I love You so much I can hardly contain it!

I lift up my family to You. Keep them safe and healthy. Be with them. Hold them up. Love them. Help them through their struggles. I cast out any depression that may linger in my family, in my house, or in me. Thank You for my family. Thank You.

Dear Lord,
I feel You working in my heart. Please be near me. Be near my family. Be near my mom. What is Your plan for her? Is she happy? Keep her joyful and in love with You. Heal her according to Your will. Seeing her sick and sad breaks my heart. My dad hurts so bad, the pain covers his face; it floods his eyes and his soul. Heal him; make him complete and whole and happy again. Amen.

CHAPTER NINE

Surrounded

The pathway is broken and the signs are unclear
and I don't know the reason why You brought me here
but just because You love me the way that You do
I'm going to walk through the fire if You want me to
~ Ginny Owens

I wish I could say my mom's cancer was the only thing my family had to endure, but unfortunately, that was not the case. In our family, when it rained, it poured.

I think our family considered ourselves to be strong, but as tragedy struck our family, it seemed we weren't that strong at all. Well, at least that's what it felt like. We all dealt with things differently, usually the wrong way, simply because we didn't know how else to deal. My dad was and is a great man, but dealing with the thought of losing his partner, his best friend, was too much for him to bear. There were days when it seemed I was not only watching my mom slip away but my dad as well.

—

I was seventeen years old. I was fast asleep in my bed when the phone rang. I answered a little groggy, and the voice on the other end sadly explained that my dad had been in a terrible accident. The voice on the other end informed me that while my dad was at work fixing a conveyer belt, he had gotten his hand stuck. He was on the top rung of the ladder trying to fix it when his fingers got caught. He panicked and kicked the ladder out from under him, leaving him dangling by only his fingers. He radioed for help but, in his panic, he didn't tell his location. It took several minutes for the other workers to find where he was and get him down. The voice on the other end told me he was badly injured, and they needed me to come to the hospital immediately. I sat in bed for a moment trying to absorb what I just heard, and then I jumped out of bed, dressed as quickly as I could, and drove as fast as I could to the hospital. I felt so sad and so worried for my dad, but I wasn't really surprised—chaos felt normal to me. When I arrived at the hospital, my dad was in bad shape. He was looking at gangrene and possibly losing his fingers. They needed to helicopter him to a bigger hospital in Vancouver for surgery. The doctors told us it would be very helpful if a family member went down with him because he would need a lot of care after his surgery. Because my mom was not capable of going, it was decided that I would go and take care of him. I went to my house to pack for two weeks away from home. I got to the house and packed all the stuff I could in the short amount of time I had before I rushed off to be with my dad. I sat on the outside step waiting for my ride to drive me to Vancouver.

As I waited, a friend came to the house because she heard what happened and wanted to see if I was all right and if I needed anything before I left. As we started talking, I began to cry. As I was talking to her, I lost it. I started yelling and crying even harder. "My family never gets a break. The bad just keeps on coming! It hurts, it hurts!" For twenty minutes, I unloaded the burdens of my heart to my dear friend. She listened and cried right along with me. After my much-needed meltdown, I caught my ride and headed to where I was needed. I gathered all the strength I could and did what I had to. Leaving meant that my fourteen-year-old brother Matthew was left to watch our mom along with a friend of mine who would stay at our house while we were gone. At that time, our mom was feeling all right, but she was still having seizures regularly and not always thinking clearly, so it was not safe for her to be left alone.

In Vancouver, I sat by my father's bedside every day with his hand tightly in mine. I talked with him and sang to him to keep him calm through the pain and the effects of the medications.

I helped with things he couldn't do on his own, like zip his coat, tie his shoes, and shave. I was there to comfort him when he was afraid and in pain. For days, he was not himself. There were times when the nurses would have to call me at my hotel and get me to come to the hospital and calm him down because the pain was so great, and he wouldn't let the nurses change his bandages without me there.

For a week, my dad was so delirious from the pain and the drugs, he would often gaze out at the view of the city and talk about the dinosaurs and gladiators waging war outside his window. So, I would spend almost every night with his hand in mine singing him to sleep. After he would fall asleep, I would walk four blocks in the big city by myself to my hotel. I was lonely, and I was scared. I desperately wanted somebody by my side. The fear I felt was paralyzing. I was scared of how hurt my dad was and scared to lose him. Our family just couldn't survive without him. I could not take care of everything all on my own.

A year went by and my dad had six surgeries on his right hand and his little finger was amputated. All this took place eight hours away from where we lived. And each time he went for surgery, I went with him to care for him. In those times, we had to be more than our parents' children. The roles were reversed, even just for a short time. Because just like we needed them, they needed us.

❧

A year and a half later, Matthew found that he was having a hard time breathing. His chest was always hurting, and he didn't know why. He was fifteen and really scared that something was terribly wrong. He had numerous doctor visits and x-rays, but they found nothing. Then an x-ray technician found something the doctor missed. They found a spot on his lung. His lung was on the verge of collapsing and that's what was causing him so much discomfort. The doctors decided he needed surgery immediately. My dad drove him four hours to the hospital where the surgery was scheduled. I met them there later to offer my support and to help care for Matthew. Matthew was and still is a very important part of my life. He was my best friend, and I felt like I had to be with him while he was going through such a scare.

With all of us gone, we relied on a friend of mine, who was a nursing student, to look after my mom for the couple of days we were away. Matthew's surgery went off without a hitch. After the surgery, he was sore and groggy, but we were told he would be as good as new.

While we were at the hotel getting some rest, we got a call in the middle of the night from my friend informing us she had just called 911, and that my mom had an abnormally long seizure and was on her way to the hospital. Almost immediately, my dad got in his car and drove the four hours back home. I urged him to get some rest first, but he just wouldn't wait. I stayed to keep an eye on Matthew and drive him back home after he was discharged.

My brother and I arrived home to discover that our mom had slipped into yet another coma. So, we went from one hospital to another in a matter of hours. Matthew and I were both so tired and worn out, especially Matthew since he just had surgery. But it didn't matter how we felt, we spent every moment by her side.

It took two weeks for her to completely come out of her coma. And like always, we brought her back home.

Not every second of every day was hectic, but whenever things were quiet, that usually just meant there was a storm ahead.

———

Things were somewhat peaceful and still for a short time. But the stillness filled us with fear and anticipation of what was about to happen. My mom caught a bad virus that was highly contagious. She was admitted to the hospital for what seemed to be the millionth time. She was under quarantine and had to stay in a room all by herself, and anyone who went in there had to wear a mask, gloves and gown.

At the same time, my grandma (my mom's mom) was admitted too. In fact, their rooms were just across the hall from each other. My grandma had been sick for some time, and she was nearing the end. With neither of them wanting to be left alone, my dad, my brother, some extended family, and I went back and forth from room to room.

One night, my dad was asleep in my grandma's room, and he heard a nurse yell his name multiple times. So he jumped up and followed the shouting into his wife's room, and as he entered her room, he found his wife barely breathing, barely hanging onto her life.

The doctor looked at him and told him to prepare himself—his wife might not make it.

The next morning, the doctor pulled my dad and me aside and told us that my mom was not stable, that she was doing very badly. I remember asking the doctor, "Is she dying?"

The doctor replied, "Yes, she is."

But of course, against all odds, Mom recovered, and we brought her home, just like we always did.

Even though the doctors were usually wrong about my mother's recovery, it was so hard to hear them tell us time and time again that she was not going to make it. She came so close to death so many times, but then she would make a complete turnaround.

⌒

Life for our family was never easy. It was often difficult to delight in the small joys. We would go for walks as a family and often my mom would collapse on the road and start to seize. Candles on a birthday cake would get blown out and everyone would be smiling and laughing until we would notice our mother's blank stare and shaking body. Many birthdays and holidays ended in hospital visits. We often felt like we couldn't ever just be happy—not even for a moment. Sometimes it felt like happiness was a warning sign for the tragedy ahead. Life was always coming at us full force.

That life got tiring. It was draining. It brings tears to my eyes every time I think of what we went through as a family.

Sometimes in life you come to a place where there is nothing but fire all around you. And the only way you make it out is to walk straight through it. You may get burned, and it may leave scars, but the fire will refine you, make you tougher, and make you strong.

Sometimes you have to go through something awful to get to somewhere good.

CHAPTER TEN

What Love Looks Like

I just never say it enough before it's too late and time's up
gift of God above, I just never say it enough
~ Wayne Watson

On September 28, 1980, my parents started their life together as husband and wife.

They stood up with their friends and exchanged vows, and they knew that with each other and with God, they could face the worst of times and make it through. The day they got married was not a glamorous one. It was at their home church in the small town where they lived, no family, just two close friends attended as their witnesses, and my mother wore a simple white dress. There was no big fancy ceremony or dazzling reception, just two people in love, just two people who wanted to start their lives together. They took all their focus and put it toward what really mattered—each other and the life they were about to share.

The vows they exchanged that day my father took to heart. "In good times and in bad, in sickness and in health, till death do us part." To my dad, those vows were more than just words. They were promises he intended to keep. In time he would prove it.

─────

Now my parents' marriage was never perfect. It had its rough moments, like most marriages do. Many years after they got married and before her diagnosis, my parents' marriage hit a breaking point. It had reached a point where all they did was argue. Fighting consumed them, and their love seemed to be fading away. My mother's past had wounded her so deeply, and she often took it out on her husband. Every little mistake he made devastated her because it reminded her of past hurts. She was terrified of being hurt like before. Even though my dad never gave her any reason to doubt him, she did. She reached a point in life where she was ruled by fear and her insecurities. Every breath, every word was driven by those things.

They were quickly drowning in my mother's anger and sadness and got to a place where they forgot why they were together; fear was ruling my mom and my dad was struggling to deal with it all. He knew she was not really angry at him, but it was directed his way nonetheless. He knew she had great reasons to act and feel the way she did, but it still hurt. My mom tried so hard to protect herself from getting hurt, and in the process, she ended up hurting the one she loved the most, the one who would never leave her. The overwhelming fear of being abandoned was pushing my father toward the door. Giving in to her fears was causing them to come true. After all of their struggles, divorce seemed like the only option. Divorce seemed to be the thing to do when things got hard in their friends' and families' marriages. Even though my parents were tempted to go that route, they knew that marriage was not supposed to be easy, and divorce would be going against everything they believed. They were not give-up-and-move-on kind of people, but they were at a complete loss and did not know what to do. Past hurts came flooding back, and they often took their pain out on each other. The tumors that they didn't know my mom had were affecting the way she acted toward her children and her husband. It affected their marriage greatly. He did not know why his wife was acting so differently, and he was at a loss for what to do about it. She yelled all the time, was always angry, always crying; some of this was due to her past and some due to the illness she did not know she had. When my mom came home with the news that she had cancer, nothing else seemed to matter to my dad; all the things they were once mad about seemed petty and unimportant. Ever argument, every disagreement they had just faded away. All that mattered was getting through the cancer—together. Life was certainly hard for them, but living a life without his wife was inconceivable for my dad. In fact, my mother's illness made him appreciate her even more. It opened his eyes. My dad devoted himself completely to my mom. He never left her side. He was there through every step and his hand never left hers. And along the way, they worked out their differences and grew closer to each other. They still struggled and fought, but through all the turmoil, their relationship grew stronger. Their love was true, their love was from God, and that could not fail.

My dad was a thoughtful and romantic husband. He was always blessing my mom with small gifts, and he remembered every anniversary. I remember a particular present my dad gave my mom when I was young. As he handed her the nicely wrapped box, my mom was puzzled as to why she was receiving a gift. Then she opened it to find a gold bracelet with a gold heart in the center and engraved on the back was the date "Dec. 18." That was the date my parents first met. He could never forget the day that he met the love of his life. Even though life was handing them unexpected changes, their love blossomed instead of withered.

Even when my mom was very sick and not always in her right mind, she still tried her best to be a loving and romantic wife. It was my dad's birthday, and my mom wanted to do something nice for her husband. My dad loved gardening, so she wanted to take him to a greenhouse to buy him a flower for his garden. He was so touched, so both of them jumped in the car and headed to the greenhouse. My dad was busy looking at all the beautiful flowers. When he turned around, he saw that his wife was having a seizure, and while she was having this seizure, he noticed a flower gripped tightly in her hand. She had found the perfect flower for her beloved husband, and no matter what, she was not going to let go.

When my mom reached her sickest and she had become a different person, no longer the woman my dad married, he would get asked the same question again and again. "Do you still love her?" And every time without pause, he would respond, "I love her more now than I ever have." It never mattered that she had changed or that she was sick. She was his wife and that's all there was to it.

Many times, I would glance over at my parents and they would be holding hands or stealing kisses from each other. When my dad would come home from a hard day at work, he would lay his head on her lap, exhausted, and she would take her hand and stroke his head. She couldn't always express herself with words, but she found a way to show him her love. Whenever she could manage a couple of words to speak, she would almost always say, "I love you, Chris," as she stared deep into his eyes. My mom slowly became dependent on my dad for her every need, and he gladly cared for her. He carried her around, bathed her, dressed her, fed her, and most of all, loved her unconditionally. Where most men would have run far away or put her in a home, my dad stayed by her side and poured more love on her than he ever had before. He became blind to the sickness, and all he saw was all her beauty. He didn't see the cancer; he just saw his wife. Nothing could change the way he felt for her. If anything, all they had been through together made him love her more.

Matthew and I just sat back and watched their love story unfold, and as we watched our parents, we hoped for a love like theirs one day.

One day, during one of the many times my mother was in the hospital, my dad went to visit her. He walked into her room and gave his wife a kiss, and she looked up at him and said, with a confused look on her face, "Who are you?"

"What?" my dad sadly replied.

"Who are you?"

Without saying a word, my dad put my mom in a wheelchair and took her to an empty room. He grabbed her hand and asked, "Who am I?"

"I don't know," she answered.

My dad held her firmly, shook her gently, and yelled, with tears falling down his face, "We made a pact! You promised me! You promised you would never leave me, that you would never forget me. We made a pact!"

And in that moment, my mom blinked her eyes a couple of times, turned to her husband, smiled and said, "Oh ... honey, hi."

"Who am I?" my dad asked.

"You're Chris, my husband." And with tears of relief streaming from his eyes, he held his wife close.

Daily my dad fought for his beloved wife, and he held onto her with all his heart and strength. He would never leave her, and she tried with all her might not to leave him. And when she started to slip away, she always came back to him. My dad never for one second stopped fighting for his wife. Every day seemed to be a battle. The fight against the illness, the fight against the depression, the fight with her mind, and one of the hardest, the battle with the doctors. My father and the doctors did not always agree on what was best for my mother. When my mother would drift into one of her comas, she would always become so sick, and it always seemed like she would not make it. My dad refused to sign a DNR (do not resuscitate order) because he knew in his heart it was not her time to go. The doctors did not understand this. They did not understand any of the decisions my dad made. In the last year of my mom's life, the doctors wanted to pull her off fluids and oxygen, and my dad said no. They thought he was so cruel not to make it easier for her to die. The doctors disagreed with my dad so much that one of them pulled my mother off fluids and oxygen against my dad's wishes. If a nurse didn't warn my dad, we could have lost her before we should have. My father never cared what they thought they knew; she wasn't done yet, and he knew what was best for his wife. His decisions were usually the right ones, and she would recover and return home. If he did not fight for her like he did, she might not have. At the point where my mother was no longer able to eat, my dad insisted a feeding tube be inserted into my mother's stomach. The doctors again disagreed with his decision. They would tell him there was no point. My dad would bluntly tell them to shut up and do as he asked. That feeding tube gave her eight more months, and during those months, she had lucid moments, and we were able to say goodbye.

In early 2007, my dad decided on early retirement, so he could take care of his beloved wife full-time. This way, he could spend every waking hour with the love of his life. He did not want to spend one more second apart. He knew in his heart that they did not have a lot of time left, and what they did have, he wanted to spend together.

When my mom died, a part of him did too. Sick or not, she was his whole world.

He didn't know how to go on living without her. I went with my dad to my mom's grave one evening years after she passed. We brought roses to plant beside her gravestone. When we got there, the gravestone was overgrown with grass and weeds. In an instant, my dad dropped to his knees and started plucking the grass from around his wife's grave. I bent down and started to help him. He said to me without looking up, "I just want to take care of her. When people look at her grave, I want them to know that she is loved."

Even though his wife is gone, he still has a longing to care for her. Even with her gone, his love has never faded, not even a little.

Letters of Love

(Journal entries and letters written by Kathleen)

Now I come before you not knowing where to start. Because in my relationship with Chris, I am very confused, and I know what I am supposed to do, but I can't get past my feelings. How can I love and respect a man who has lied to me all our married life? How do I get rid of these feelings of betrayal? At the same time, I acknowledge my sin of not being a good wife. I just think life should be happier even among trials. Every time I look in the mirror it's hard to look at myself. I feel I'm ageing so fast! I'm tired all the time! Lord, I don't know what else to say but "HELP ME JESUS!" I rebuke and I bind the spiritual forces that are trying to break up my marriage, be gone spirit of adultery, be gone spirit of lust, be gone spirit of divorce! Satan, leave my family alone! Leave me alone! Jesus help me through this day this next week. I want to do what Your Word says not just hear it. Change me Lord. I'll let You worry about Chris.

In Jesus' name!
Amen

Lord, I ask you to give me love for Chris, make it brand new, better than before. Amen

September 1986
Today is our anniversary of six years: Chris took me to a wonderful dinner last night and lavished gifts upon me. He is becoming such a loving and thoughtful person. Thank you, Jesus!

Today Chris and I did the Sunday school together and again the Lord came through, and it turned out pretty good.

November 1992
Heavenly Father,

I don't pretend to have the answers as far as Chris and I are concerned. I cannot help how I feel. One thing I do know is that it is Your will for our marriage to work. It is Your will for us to be happy, it is your will for us to have love and enjoy one another—then let Your will be done. Thy kingdom come Thy will be done in our marriage. Amen.

Chris,
Happy Anniversary. Sometimes it's hard to say what's really on your mind. So in this poem I will write my feelings of every kind.

I love you for your thoughtfulness and your kind and loving ways.
I love you because you work so hard only thinking of us each day.
I love you when you make me smile when I'm sad and feeling low,
I love how you say you love me; I know it must be so!
Listen and I will share with you a thought I hold so clear,
I love you, Chris, I will love you, through each and every year

We've had our ups and downs, and we've had our downs in this last year together, and do you know something? I wouldn't change a minute of it, even if I could. It may not seem like it sometimes, but I do care for you, very deeply. I hope that this year has meant as much to you as it has to me.

With all my love, Kathy

(Journal entries written by Maralee)

September 28, 2005
It was my parents' anniversary today. My dad loves my mom so much. He gives new meaning to the words love and romance. He does the gross, hard, sad things. He goes far beyond what any husband would. It's easy

to write love songs, buy roses, and be mushy, but what about bathing your wife, changing her, putting diapers on her, cleaning up after her. That may be gross, but that to me is romantic and true, real never-ending love. I want that kind of love. I want to love and be loved like that. They are an inspiration, not just to me and Matthew, but to everyone who knows them. They deserve the world, blessings from Heaven; they deserve the best.

Dear God,
Bless my parents. Help them forget their worries, pain, and tragedies and focus on their love and what You have in store for them. Give them hope, strength, and another twenty-five years. Pour out all you've got on the greatest two people I have ever known. You are so lucky you get to see their hearts; it must be a beautiful sight. Thanks for my parents. I'm truly blessed. Amen.

CHAPTER ELEVEN

Whispers

Your prayer has been heard; the answer is on
its way. It is a most unusual answer
and it's coming from the most unexpected source.
~ Source Unknown

When it came to my mother's illness, everyone was waiting on a miracle. They would pray for God to heal her, for Him to make her mind whole again, for everything to go back to the way it once was. My dad's church would hold prayer meetings that were solely devoted to my mother and her healing. People talked like her "healing" would take place any day. Everyone was so certain that she would overcome her illness, and it would be like the cancer never happened. These people prayed and believed with such intensity that it was sometimes frightening.

They would not even entertain the thought that her physical healing may not come. I admired their belief and faith, but I myself took a different approach to it all. I was not at all certain of anything. I did not know for a fact that my mother would be "healed". Although I knew with my whole heart that God was powerful enough to heal her, I was just not sure if that was His will, but I hoped with all that I had that it was. But I wrestled with the question of why my mom's healing wouldn't be God's will. Why wouldn't He want her healed and our family whole? I couldn't understand it and it deeply confused me. I still struggle to comprehend it. But I had to accept that things were out of my control and trust there was a purpose.

Instead of praying for a huge miracle (though I would be lying if I said I didn't pray for that sometimes too), I prayed for something different. I was incredibly tired and worn. Towards the end, I prayed wholeheartedly, "Do what you need to do, and I will trust it." This change of heart and prayer took so much pressure off me and gave me a sense of peace. Sadly, we never saw the miracle everyone was praying for come to light. For some, that meant that God didn't hear our prayers; for some, that meant that our family failed because we didn't pray hard enough or believe hard enough, but I know that none of that is true. God gave us our miracles, just not the one everyone was hoping for. People just didn't count them because they seemed small and insufficient; they wanted a big miracle, but in my opinion, there is no such thing as a small miracle. Max Lucado wrote in his book, *In the Eye of the Storm*, "Because we look for the bonfire, we miss the candle. Because we listen for the shout, we miss the whisper." When we bring our problems to God, we often expect some huge answer, some great response to our prayers. We look so hard for some huge miracle that we miss the small and simple whispers. The miracles we as a family experienced throughout the years changed our lives greatly, and they gave us just what we needed when we needed it.

We were given friends we could call on at a moment's notice, friends we could count on. The times when we would be at the hospital with our mom, we would usually end up eating nothing but chips, cookies, and pop, so friends from my dad's church would bring us home-cooked meals every night until my mom was sent home. We always had good friends who we could vent to and cry with. We couldn't walk through the valley alone, and God made sure we didn't.

However, with everyone's attention on my mom and her health, it often became lonely for me. I often felt invisible and uncared for. I had reached a low point in my life, and I really needed somebody. I needed to be seen. I needed an ear to hear me and a shoulder to cry on. Then I met James. He quickly became my best friend and was there for me every second that I needed him; he never left my side. James helped me take care of my mom. He would help lift her in and out of bed; he would do whatever my dad or I needed. We would even take her on outings together. On my lowest of days, he would pick up my slack and take care of everything. When my mom was in the hospital, he would go visit her on his own when I was unable to.

He was everything I needed and more. He looked past my hurt and sadness and he loved me unconditionally—something I had never experienced before. He saw me at my worst, at my most broken, and he never left; his love for me never changed. When my mom passed, I had someone to hold my hand and to hold me close when I broke down, someone to carry some of my heavy load. In the midst of my taking care of my family, he took care of me, and I needed that more than anything. I am not sure if I could have gotten through that loss without him.

I married James in 2006, and against all odds, my mother got to see it. The doctors said she would not make it three years, but she made it twelve and got to see her only daughter walk down the aisle.

During the day of my wedding, I was a little unsure if she really knew what was going on, if she really understood that her baby girl was getting married. My dad kept having to tell her that it was me who was getting married, but I tried so hard not to focus on that. I was just glad she was there and that she was able to celebrate with me.

I got to share one of the happiest days of my life with my mother, even though I was told I probably wouldn't get to. That day my whole family was together. Aunts, uncles, grandparents, my brothers—we were all together. At the time we didn't know it, but that would be the last time we would all be together like that. We took pictures, laughed, danced; it was simply wonderful.

It was so great and amazing that we were given the opportunity to have some quality family time. During the reception, we had a dance. I had the absolute pleasure of sharing a dance with my beautiful mom. Later on in the evening, as I danced with my little brother, I looked over his shoulder and saw my new husband approach my mom who was seated and tapping her foot to the beat of the music. He offered his hand to her and asked her to dance; she smiled, took his hand, and followed him to the dance floor. With joy in my heart, I watched them dance together. At one point in the night, my mom dinged the wine glass during dinner for my husband and me to kiss; she had a huge grin on her face and when she did that, I knew in that moment she really understood even just for a minute what was happening, and she was happy for me. In that moment, tears trickled down my face. These beautiful moments and memories may seem small, but to me they might as well have been the whole world.

Shortly after I was married, something amazing happened. It had been quite some time since we could carry on a complete conversation with our mother and a whole year since she had spoken at all. She was often confused, and we were unsure if she knew who we were at times.

One morning I got a call at around 7:00 a.m. I answered the phone a little groggy. Suddenly, I heard the most beautiful sound I have ever heard. "It's mom. I love you and I miss you." Before I responded, I sat up straight in my bed stunned. With my left hand, I held the phone tightly to my ear and with the other I attempted to wake James, so he could hear what I was hearing. I hadn't heard my mom's voice in almost a year, and she was calling me and carrying on a conversation. We talked for about five minutes. My dad was so excited about my mom being so alert and able to communicate that he asked her to call all their family and friends. If no one answered, she would leave voice messages on their machines, which left everybody speechless!

I got up, got dressed, and ran over to my parents' house. When I got there, Matthew was sitting on her bed with our dad. She was fully alert, carrying on conversations like nothing was ever wrong. She was joking and giving parenting advice to her husband and motherly advice to us kids. My dad just sat by her bedside for days asking her questions he had been dying to ask her. In those days, she gave him her opinions and insights. After my mom spoke with my dad, you could see his load lighten. At this time, Matthew was eighteen, and he had started to experiment with his appearance. He had dyed his blond hair black, wore eyeliner, and was sporting some pretty tight pants. My dad often made his disdain for his son's new look known, but mom was unable to express her opinion, so when Matthew came up to Mom's bedside, the first thing she said to him was, "Why do you look so weird?!" Matthew smiled and laughed; he was just so happy to be talking with his mother. She must have wanted to ask that for a long time because as soon as she could speak, it was one of the first things she said to him. No matter how sick she was or what she had been through, she was a mother through and through, and no sickness could take that away.

She was alert and talking for three whole days, and we soaked up every minute of it. For a short moment in time, it was like we had never lost her. After those three days, she drifted back to what she was like before. But those days gave us a chance to talk to our mom, hear her voice, and know her thoughts, feelings, and opinions. Ultimately, it gave us a chance to say goodbye. Those days gave us something we had been wanting for. We had missed her so much, and for a minute, we got our mom back.

After that, she would occasionally break her silence even just for a moment with words of love for her husband or to tell him not to worry about her. Then she would slip back. But in those minutes, those words were just what my dad desperately needed and wanted to hear.

It was three years after my mother's passing, and I had just had my second child, a daughter. I was feeling very overwhelmed. I wanted to go to church and be involved in things, but I was not always able to because of my motherly duties. I absolutely loved being a mom, but at times, I felt overwhelmed and discouraged. I was also battling with deep sadness at the time. I just had another child and my mom was not there with me. Although I do not quite remember, my husband told me that during labor as I began to push, I looked at him and cried, "I wish my mom was here." The moment my daughter was born, there was such joy of course, but this awful sadness followed; the void I felt was so great. My mother was supposed to be there, and her hand was supposed to be in mine; she was supposed to be one of the first to hold my precious baby. What I would have given for her to be there with me, for her to hold her granddaughter. Every day after my daughter was born, I felt her absence more strongly than ever before. I made my daughter's middle name Kathleen in an effort to make her a part of my little one's life. Every time I spoke it, I was filled with joy but also sorrow. Crying was very frequent for weeks after my baby's birth. I so badly needed my mom, and I desperately wanted to hear her voice and ask her for advice. I was dealing with many things and was feeling extremely overwhelmed. My heart was filled with dreams that I couldn't quite reach and goals I felt I would ever achieve. I spent most church services with my children in the nursery, and sometimes I just felt like I was missing everything. I was drained and I could feel myself fading away. While I was feeling this way, my dad came for a visit, and he brought my mother's journals with him. One day I was cuddled up with my beautiful baby girl, rocking her to sleep, and while I was doing so, I began to read my mother's words. On the second page of her journal, I read this:

God has shown me that I must set my priorities right concerning serving those I love, i.e., God first, my husband, then my children, then the church etc.

He has also shown me today that I shouldn't feel bad if Maralee takes most of my time for He says in Mark 9:37a KJV "Whosoever receives one of such children in My name, receiveth Me." I have been feeling condemnation when I haven't attended church functions because of the care Maralee needed and I have felt that we needed to stay home. <u>My first ministry is toward my family.</u>

As soon as I read this, tears filled my eyes, and I was overcome with emotion. Even though my mom was gone, she still managed to give me advice and was able to tell me just what I needed to hear. She helped me. She reminded me how important it is to be a mother and that what I was doing was still ministry, just a different form. She reminded me I was living my dream, just of a different sort, and that my goals and dreams of my heart were not lost. I was feeling so far away from her, but then I was given something to hold on to, something that made me feel close to her again.

I don't know why God didn't heal my mom, and I don't care. I am just thankful for what He did give us. Some people waste so much energy and time wishing things were different and hoping things would change and being so angry and bitter when they don't. Being angry when things don't go the way we desperately want them to won't change anything. We just have to be thankful for what we do have and the time we have been given. I don't want to be so caught up in the things I want that I miss the precious moments handed to me. God gave us everything we needed. He gave us time when we were told that time was up. When we were at our breaking point, He gave us strength to carry on.

CHAPTER TWELVE

An Inspiration to All

When peace, like a river, attendeth my way,
When sorrows like sea billows roll;
Whatever my lot, Thou has taught me to say,
It is well; it is well, with my soul.
~ Horatio Spafford

It was the middle of September 2007, and I was nine months pregnant with my first child. I was at my parents' house, like most evenings, spending time with my mom and helping my dad take care of her. It started to get late and my dad went off to bed. As the night passed, I went into my mom's room to check on her, and I noticed she would have moments where she wouldn't be breathing. I sat down by her bed to see if her breathing would improve. I didn't want to wake my dad up and get him upset or worried for nothing. But her breathing was not improving; in fact, it seemed to be getting worse. So, with a heavy and frightened heart, I reluctantly woke up my dad, knowing that every time she gets sick it breaks his heart. He walked into my mother's room, took a look at his barely conscious wife, bent over, and put his ear to her chest. He stood up and gently brushed her hair with his hands and calmly told me to call 911. I rushed into the room where the phone was and made the call. The paramedics arrived quickly and took my mother to the hospital. Normally I would go with her to the hospital but this time it was 1:00 a.m. and I was nine months pregnant, so my husband encouraged me to stay home and get some rest. After some protest, I agreed to stay and go in the morning.

Shortly after she arrived at the hospital, she slipped into her fourth and final coma. This hospital visit seemed no different from all the others, but little did we know, it was.

Over the past nine months, I had talked to my mom about the upcoming birth of my new baby, and she would rub and kiss my belly. My mom was able to come to my baby shower, which thrilled me. When I was little, I just assumed that I would share these moments with my mom. I always thought that she would be in the delivery room when I had my children. But as I got older and life took over and my mother became sicker and sicker, I realized all the things I pictured in my mind probably wouldn't come to pass. Even though the circumstances changed, I still hoped to share all I could with my mom. I imagined helping her hold my baby and her kissing her grandchild on the forehead. When she went into her coma, I was so scared that she would not make it to meet my baby. I was so terrified that she would die just before I was supposed to give birth and that I would not have the strength to do it without her.

Two weeks after she had gone into the coma, I had given birth to a beautiful baby boy. We were both in separate hospitals, so when I was discharged, my husband and I jumped in the car and drove directly to the hospital where my mom was. We walked as fast as we could into her room. I felt like I was in a race against time and I was losing. I was so afraid that my baby would not get to meet his grandma. We walked into the room and my dad came over and kissed his new grandson. My mom was still unconscious, but I was determined that my son and my mom would at least be in each other's presence. I took my sleeping son out of his car seat and placed him in his grandma's arms. And for a short time, they just laid together peacefully. The sight of them together warmed my heart because I knew then that even if she died, at least she got to hold her grandson. We named our precious son Isaac. The name Isaac means laughter. This little bundle was a bright light in the darkness. When someone was crying and grief-stricken, we would carry Isaac into the room and he instantly put smiles on people's faces and his little noises often filled the room with laughter. Although it felt overwhelming at times, that little boy was what we needed. He was a miracle in so many ways. He was something happy at a time of sadness.

Two more weeks passed. I was sitting at home in my living room nursing my baby. I was looking down at my beautiful baby boy, stroking his sweet little head. I remember thinking, "I am so incredibly happy." Seconds after that thought, the phone rang. A shaky, quiet voice greeted me on the other end. It was my dad. "She's gone," he said. "She passed away."

"What?" I quietly replied. I remember thinking, "Is this a joke?" On one hand, I was prepared. My mother had been sick for a long time. We were told tons of times that she wouldn't make it through the night. But on the other hand, I was shocked. We may have been told she wouldn't make it so many times, but each time she did. She came home every single time. I could not believe that this time she wouldn't. Moments after I hung up the phone, Matthew burst through my front door and landed face first on my kitchen floor, crying uncontrollably. I was still nursing Isaac, so I asked my husband to go and comfort him. As they held each other and cried, I held my newborn baby close and cried along with them.

Our hearts were broken. At the age of fifty-three, our mom was gone. My husband drove us both to the hospital to say goodbye and to be with our dad. As we drove to the hospital, I had my left hand in my husband's hand and my right reached around to the backseat tightly holding my brother's. As we all sat quietly, a song came on by Sara Groves called "It's Going to be Alright."

I believe you'll outlive this pain in your heart
And you'll gain such a strength from what is tearing
you apart
Oh, oh I believe I believe that

It's going to be alright
It's going to be alright

When some time has passed us, and the story is retold
It will mirror the strength and the courage in your soul

As we listened to those words, tears welled in our eyes. I tightly closed my eyes and let those words settle deep within my heart, so as the years went on, and I missed my mother terribly, I could hold on to those words and know in my soul that everything was going to be alright.

The car pulled up to the hospital and Matthew and I got out. We slowly started walking toward the hospital doors, blankly staring up at that huge building. Matthew reached for my hand, and we began the longest walk of our lives. That walk to my mother's hospital bed felt so surreal. I remember looking at my brother saying, "I can't believe this is it," and him softly shaking his head in disbelief. We walked into our mom's room, and as soon as we saw her face, her eyes closed and body lifeless, we started to cry harder than before. Our crying was so intense; it was physically painful. I laid down in bed beside her, placing my head on her chest and holding her hand in mine, and Matthew laid his body across her feet and we just held her and cried. My grandpa was standing by her bedside, with grief written all over his face. My dad was in the corner, staring at the floor, sobbing. Once the crying slowed down, I just sat by her bedside with her hand clutched tightly in mine and I stared at her. She looked so peaceful. As awful as it was to have her leave us, she had been in pain for years and her body and mind had been through so much, so I was comforted by the fact that she was now at rest.

Even So

I had the hardest time leaving her room that night because I knew it would be the last time I would ever see her. I could not bear the thought of never seeing my mother again. I would start to walk away, but then quickly turn back and grab her hand. My husband and I were the last ones to leave her room that night. I just could not bring myself to leave her. But I finally got up the courage, and I kissed her on the cheek and whispered in her ear, "I love you. Goodbye, mommy." As I turned to leave, I saw James lean in and whisper in my mother's ear and kiss her on the cheek. He walked over to me and grasped my hand. As I walked down the hall of the hospital, tears poured down my face, and I fought the urge to run back into my mother's room. I could not believe I would never see my mom ever again. Walking away from her that night, saying goodbye, was heart-wrenching and one of the hardest things I have ever done.

That night we sat in the living room of my parents' house. Oddly enough our tears had stopped for the moment. We just talked about how great our mom was. We laughed as we reminisced about her life. We found some comfort in each other's company and stories. The next week was a whirlwind. I looked after my newborn, who was just two weeks old, while at the same time planning my mom's funeral. It was hectic and overwhelming. I was completely exhausted and worn.

My parent's house was full of people, aunts, uncles, grandparents, siblings, and friends. It was busy and overwhelming. They all had opinions and suggestions, well-intended but exhausting. Tensions were high. There were many arguments between various people usually about nothing of importance. Everywhere you looked there were people; there was nowhere to be alone. That time was stifling and claustrophobic. My dad especially was a mess after my mother died. Members of his family kept trying to get him to hold Isaac, but he never wanted to. He could barely look at him. In part he was scared because he felt so unstable; he was worried he might drop him. For months he stayed in the house. Hiding. He didn't want to leave the safety of his home. One time I asked him to go somewhere with me and with tear-filled eyes he told me, "I can't. I cannot bear to watch these people driving around, grocery shopping, getting coffee, going to work. How can life carry on as usual? Don't they know my wife is dead?" I was sad for my dad's breaking heart and sad because I felt the same way. Our world as we knew it ended, and for everyone else on earth, it was like business as usual, and that was gut-wrenching.

The funeral was held a week later. It was a joyful celebration of her life.

Of course, we were sad to say goodbye, but we celebrated our mother's wonderful spirit and inspirational life. All three of her kids sang at her funeral. Brian sang "Amazing Grace," I sang the hymn, "It Is Well," and Matthew closed the service with a song he wrote especially for her. We wanted to honour our mother with song since that was one of things she loved so much. When we sang that night, it was not just to fill time in the service. We sang for her, with everything we had, we each sang one more song for our mom. I gave my mother's eulogy that night and told of her strength and love. I encouraged people not to remember only her sickness but to remember the wonderful, talented person she was. She was much more than her illness. She was a woman of great faith and conviction. The service was beautiful and joyful, just like she was. It was a funeral like no one had experienced before.

After it was over, I spent at least an hour listening to everyone's condolences, feeling so sad and tired and desperately wanting the day to be over. A woman my mom had known a very long time came up to me and sat down beside me. She complimented me on my song and said, "Your mother was right about you."

"Right about what?" I asked.

She looked at me and said, "I once offered your mother a

compliment on her singing voice and she just looked at me and said, "Thank you, but you should hear my daughter sing."

⁓

The next day, we had another service at the cemetery where she was to be buried. My brothers and I stood at the empty grave hand in hand, with tears of grief falling down our faces. I watched my brothers help carry her casket, and I watched as Matthew stumbled and fought the urge not to break down. I watched as she was lowered into the grave where the gravestone would read "An Inspiration to All," and I was suddenly hit with the reality of it. It seemed so final now. She was really gone. That feeling overtook me. I could feel my breath slipping away from me, my legs started to fail me, and I felt too weak to stand. As I started to fall, my husband wrapped his arms around me and helped me stand. I completely leaned into him and depended on him to keep me standing. Because my strength was failing me, I relied on his.

The sadness I felt that day is indescribable. The feeling of never seeing her again was devastating. But then I was reminded that the body that was being lowered into the ground was no longer my mom. That was just flesh and bones. What made my mom beautiful, brave, strong, and amazing was her spirit—and that was very much alive. One day I will see her again, and when I do, she will be whole, healed, and happy, and that simple truth gives me peace.

⁓

Many people thought because God didn't heal my mom, we lost. But I think the opposite.

I believe God did heal my mom, just not in the way we would have thought or wanted. As I write this, she is in the most beautiful place, and she is whole and complete. She is no longer in pain; she is cancer-free. I believe fighting for so long and making it through is a victory in itself.

Though most people may not feel this way, we won. And I am sure my mother would agree, and if she could tell you, she would say that walking hand in hand with glory is the greatest prize. She may have lived on this earth, but this place was never her home. And now my mother is where she has always belonged. My dad always told my mom and her doctors that no matter what happened He would bring her home, and when she died, his promise wasn't broken; it just wasn't him who brought her home. I imagine that when the gates opened before her and she stood face to face with glory, she heard the words she lived her whole life for, "Well done, good and faithful servant."

Letters of Witnesses

(Letters written by friends and family)

Maralee,

Where do I start? It seems like so many years ago. Several memories are clear in my mind. One, the stabilizing effect that Kathy had on your father's life and a card that she once gave me. The stabilizing effect is and has been evident up to the time that she departed to be with Jesus. From that time, Chris has had a big part of his life gone. The card was given to me back in and around 1985. You most likely heard that I used to chew snuff (a very filthy habit). We, Nancy, I, and the children made a trip back to Fruitvale and upon our arrival, we made our way to your house on Hillcrest. When I knocked on the door, your Mother came to the door and gave me a card. The card said in it that you all loved me and did not want to lose me to a stupid, addictive, and health-destroying habit. It was not judgment, but a heartfelt concern for my well-being and the fact that she did not want to forfeit our friendship. This was taken to the point of challenging me in my self-destroying habit! It was done in Love and I knew that. Later that summer, with Nancy's encouragement and your folks' prayer, Jesus delivered me. I miss your Mom. She brought joy to our hearts, she inspired us in our faith, and she blessed us with her love and wonderful voice! What more can I say other than "precious in the sight of The Lord is the death of His chosen ones." Kathy you are missed!

In Christ,
Paul Jackson (a close family friend)

Nielsen Family,

Even though distance separates us, there are some bonds that can't be broken. I like to think that the bond I have with the Nielsen family is one of those.

Chris and Kathy impacted my life in a way that no one else has. Let me tell you about Chris first.

In the Word, we are told that husbands should love their wives as Christ loved the Church. That marriage is a picture of Christ and His bride. Chris displayed that for the world to see. I've heard stories through the years of people who have cared for their spouses through sickness and health: those who sacrificed and laid down their own lives for their spouse in caring for them through long and often intense illnesses. But I had never seen it up close and personal until I watched Chris care for Kathy. He would tell us how he had come to love her even more through those last twelve years of her life here on earth. But it wasn't just words. He proved it with every action. With being Kathy's advocate, her care giver, her nurse, fighting with the doctors, sitting by her side through every situation. I sit here, still emotionally impacted by remembering Chris' love for Kathy. I count it a true privilege to have witnessed the small portion that I did.

Kathy impacted me in a totally different way. I remember the tenacity she had in her faith. Her gentle spirit and grace towards others—regardless of who they were or how they treated her. Kathy was an inspiration to me. Her attitude—where she knew the Lord would heal her—either on this earth or in heaven. There was never a doubt in her mind.

To have known her through those years gave the opportunity to witness the changes in her physical health and body. To the world, her health digressed. The interesting part was that as her health decreased her faith increased. It was like a scale—as one side decreased, the other increased. Kathy seemed to have a giant faith.

One of the many stories that speaks of Kathy's gentle spirit was when she was approached telling her if her faith was stronger, how she would be healed. Kathy's response was not one of anger, but she asked the person to teach her to have that faith. The rest of us wanted to know who the insensitive clod was who had the audacity to say that. Anyone who 'knew'

Kathy knew that she had faith. She immersed herself in the Word early in her fight. Chris built her their worship room so that she could be immersed in worship at any time of the day or night. As far as I could see, she did everything right in order to exercise her faith. She was and is one of my heroines of the faith.

I will forever consider myself fortunate to have been her friend (as well as Chris') and to have had the opportunity to spend time with her near the end of her life here on earth. I look forward to the time when we'll meet again. Maybe I'll finally have that opportunity to sing with her.

Love,
Linda Buhler (family friend)

Nielsen Family,
I first met Kathy in September of 2001. I had heard of her challenges and her triumphs.

Kathy was the epitome of courage and grace under fire.
Just being in the room with her evoked a sense of wonder in God.
Her faith was childlike and strong.
It was always very clear that she was focused on the Lord and not on her circumstances.
She always had a twinkle in her eye as if to say "I know something you don't know" and she did ... she was deeply connected to the Father.

I will always remember the time I went to visit her on the third floor of the Kootenay Boundary Regional Hospital where she would go from time to time.

She loved worship and singing, and I held her hand and sang for to her for about forty-five minutes. I did not want to tire her out, so I stopped singing. She got this rather stern look in her eye and made a guttural sound, and it was clear that I was not done singing until she was ready for me to stop... so I continued to sing...

I will always remember the Sunday she came to church and was so touched by the worship and message that she could not contain it. We always knew when she needed to communicate something. So I went back to where she was and held her hand and tears rolled down her face as I spoke with her about the goodness of God and how he loved her.

She challenged us all with her unwavering love for God and her family. She was feisty and funny and deeply sensitive to the Spirit of God. One day she looked down at my toe ring and pointed at it. I knew that she liked it and that Christmas the elders' wives and I bought her one for Christmas. I knew then that even though she was limited in her communication she was very in tune with her surroundings.

It was the greatest honor to be with her. I was touched that she allowed me into those intimate moments she had with the Lord. I will never be the same and will carry her in my heart always.

Blessings,
Abby Pillai-Silva (Family Friend)

Dear Nielsens,
I learned so much from you. You lived in expectation of healing in the midst of pain. Maralee and I spent many evenings at your house early in our marriage. I remember a large red Bible sitting on the dining room table topped with a pair of reading glasses. A fixture more familiar to that table than food. At that table, Bible open, glasses in hand, Chris, you would tell me your notes from sermons you'd heard that struck you. I remember your mischievous grin when you were telling me some truth you had recently grasped or been grasped by. You once grinned and spoke about Daniel's friends stepping into the furnace saying, "Even so." I don't know

Even So

if I've ever come across such depth of truth as when watching you ponder this notion out loud. This idea was shared by both you and Kathy. I saw this idea expressed in both of your daily lives. This was maybe the most important thing you and Kathleen taught me.

Love,
James Mason (Son-in-law)

CHAPTER THIRTEEN

When the Silence Isn't Quiet

Peace isn't a place where there is no noise, trouble, or hard work,
it means to be in the midst of those things
and still be calm in your heart.
~ Unknown

When you lose someone you love, there are some things that overtake
you after they're gone. These things can swallow you whole and eat
you alive. My mother was my whole life. Over time my identity
began to be centered around her. She was my purpose. When I lost
my mother, I also lost myself. Every time she yelled at me, every
seizure, every hit, every coma, every time something went wrong, it
added a piece to who I was. During the last three years of her life,
almost everything I did was for her, so when she died, I felt empty,
and that's when lies crept in and tried to fill the empty spaces.
During those long years my mother was ill, everything was so loud.
Everything was so busy. Nothing was still or quiet. So when she was
gone, we looked for the stillness our souls had been longing for, but
we found only lies which spoke loudly in my mind. Things around
me were calmer, but my mind certainly wasn't.

There were four main things that plagued us the most after
Mom died.

Guilt is something I know too well. Your mind starts to fill up with all the things you didn't say, all the things you said but wish you didn't. All the things you didn't do and wish you did, and all the things you did and wish you could erase. You play these things over in your mind like a movie. And as you play it over in your mind, it is kind of like watching a horror film—where the girl is going to do something stupid like go down into the dark basement and you know she shouldn't go down there, because that's where the murderer is. And you yell out, "Don't go down there! Don't do it!" As we play our life over in our heads, we see all the stupid things we did and all the dumb and pointless things we said, and we just want to scream, "Don't do it!"

There was a point in my mother's illness when she had to use a wheelchair. She could no longer walk; her legs were too weak to hold her up. She depended on her family to take her where she needed to go. We would carry her from the car or the couch to her wheelchair. She was only ninety pounds but was heavy; her limp body made her seem heavier than she was. One night, my brother and I decided to take our mom to a movie, a cartoon (she loved those). After the movie was over, we were wheeling her to the car and we went over the curb with the chair, and she fell out onto the pavement. We both gasped and rushed to her. She was making this whimpering noise. And her face looked so scared and sad. We tried to pick her back up to put her in the chair, but we couldn't lift her high enough. It was just too hard to lift her up just the two of us; we just weren't strong enough. A friend of my brother's walked by and saw and ran to help. We tried for at least five minutes before we finally got her back in her chair. By this time, we were all crying, although Matthew and I tried to hide our tears from our mom. We finally got her in the car. I dropped my mom and brother off at home. As I pulled out of the driveway, I started to sob. I felt so awful, like the worst daughter ever. To this day I can still see her face in my mind, so sad and scared. That day still tears me up. I get bombarded with thoughts like, "I should have been more careful," "How could I let that happen," and "What kind of daughter am I?"

—

When my mom died, everything I ever did wrong flooded my mind. All the times I lost my temper with her, and all the times I yelled at her when I shouldn't have. All the times I didn't give her grace when she needed it. And most importantly, all the times I should have been there with her and wasn't. I could have done all the good in the world—it didn't matter.

I spent almost every minute in the last year of my mother's life by her side. But when she died, I couldn't remember that or any of the good I did. All I could see was all the bad. Guilt can be cruel, but with it comes grace. It acknowledges your mistakes but also makes room to try again. It makes your decisions regrettable, but not unredeemable. When I look back on that day at the movie theater, it seems like a perfect illustration of how we as a family felt every day my mom was sick. Things were so difficult, and we had to see things and deal with things that were heart-wrenching. We could not do it on our own; we just weren't strong enough. And when we were just about to give up hope, help came. Just like everything we as a family went through, we try to let our mistakes and regrets teach us. There is good in the bad; we just don't often look for it there.

Shame. It may seem similar to guilt, but it is very different. It is more ruthless and unforgiving. It attacks the very essence of who you are. It yells that you are not enough and insists you are your mistakes. It convinces you that there is nothing you can do to change it.

I was embarrassed for others to know my "secrets". After the passing of my mother, my family would look back on that difficult time and it would tear us apart. We could see clearly now that we didn't always do the right thing; we started to remember all the wrong things we did, and we dwelt on those. A year after my mom's passing, I moved away and I met new people, and for the longest time, I would not and could not tell them about my mom and what I had been through. I was ashamed. I was so focused on all the wrong I did back then that I overlooked the good my story could cause. I was too ashamed of my scars and who I used to be. Before my mother died, I did turn things around, but that didn't matter. All I could remember was all the harm I did. I felt like if I revealed where I came from or the things I had done or who I used to be, then people would see me differently; they would no longer see the person I had become. When my mom was sick and when I was going through my depression, everyone around me looked at me different. I often felt judged and misunderstood and I didn't want to feel that way again, especially after I had worked so hard to change and overcome my circumstances. I feared my past could undo the changes I had made. Then I was reminded of a story a pastor once told in one of his sermons. It was a story of a girl who suffered greatly with depression. She went through a terrible time where the pain was so severe that she cut herself. She would take a knife and slice into the skin of her arm. After some time and hard work, that girl overcame her sadness. But now that she was healed, she was ashamed of the scars on her arms. She did not want anyone to see them, and she didn't want to see them herself. They just reminded her of what she went through. So, she would wear long-sleeved shirts to cover them up. She shared her feelings about her scars with the pastor, and he told her to be proud of them and not to hide them—they showed how far she had come. Scars are wounds that have healed. They were a great reminder of who she used to be and who she wants to be. Those scars are not marks of a failure, but marks of someone who has overcome.

That story has taught me so much, and I have carried it with me ever since. My past doesn't have to be a burden that holds me back. It can be a tool that continues to help me grow and perhaps help others as well. My wounds, my scars, and my pain show who I used to be, but they also show how far I have come. They tell my story, and it is a story that should be told, no matter how upsetting it can be or how much it reminds me of all the pain my family and I have endured. I now wear my scars proudly, and I try to tell my story without shame.

People were always taken aback at my mother's candor. And people were the same way when I started writing this book. Not many people like their secrets exposed and their mistakes talked about, but my mother was not one of those people. My mother was never afraid to tell her story. She was never afraid to share the details of her struggles, no matter how gory. After receiving Christ, she felt it was her calling to tell anyone and everyone her story. She wanted to use her past to help others in their futures. I have often heard people say, "When I die, I want people only to remember the good, not the bad." But my mom didn't want people to remember her as perfect because what can someone learn from a perfect person? She wanted people to see all of her, her entire story, the good and the bad, the right choices and the wrong ones. No one would know how far she came if they didn't know where she had been. No one would know what God had done for her, if they didn't know what she overcame. My mother hid nothing from the world. She would get up in front of hundreds of people and tell of her past. She told of her abortion, hoping it would help heal a woman who went through the same thing. She told of her drinking and drug use unashamed because she knew she was forgiven. Growing up, I knew it all. Even from a young age, my parents did not hide who they used to be from us. They would use their past as a tool to help teach us. To help us make different choices.

People always say leave the past in the past. But I don't believe that is possible. My dad once told me, "You can't really leave the past behind you. The past is a part of who you are. It goes where you go; it is what has made you who you are. All you can do is accept your past as truth and make your peace with it and move onward." It is not much of an accomplishment to seem perfect and mistake-free, but it is absolutely inspiring to be a person who has made mistakes, felt pain and heartache, and overcame it all.

Blame weaseled its way into our thoughts as well. My mom's sickness and death seemed so unfair. It often made things easier to blame someone for the agony we were feeling. Blame was a way we could try to make sense of it all. Blame can be two things—a convenient and often untruthful way to rewrite our story so we are not the villain, or proof that we are indeed the bad guy.

My brother Matthew aimed most of his blame toward God. Why would a loving God let this happen? We are a good family, we served and loved Him, and this is how He treats us? It did not make sense to him. Why did He have to take her? He doesn't need her—we do. For a long time, Matthew wrestled with this, and in a way, we all did.

We were also so quick to blame each other, the ones closest to us. We often took notice in detail of each other's mistakes, more than our own. We memorized them, as they distracted us from our own mistakes.

The people we blamed the most were ourselves. Just before my mother's death, my dad really struggled and gave in to the lie that if she died it would be because he didn't pray hard enough because his faith wasn't strong enough. After she died, we were consumed with "what ifs" and "maybes". What if we held her hand more? What if I went to church more? Maybe we could have made her last months more enjoyable; maybe we could have been there more for her and for each other; maybe we could have been stronger; maybe we could have prayed more, believed more. We could have drowned in all the maybes. It was easier to make up a reason or to point fingers instead of admitting and accepting the truth, that there is no reason and that there is no one to blame, no one at all.

After my mother's death, my family also faced **Fear.** Fear had always played a role in our lives—fear for my father's breaking heart, for my parents' overall well-being, and fear of losing them both or fear of losing each other. We used fear as a shield to protect us from any more heartache, but then it became a barrier that stopped us from truly living.

When we lost my mother, the fear we experienced intensified a hundred times. We were so used to terrible things happening that we came to expect them. It was our normal. So even with my mom gone, we were always waiting for something bad to happen. It was the life we had always known. For the longest time, we never let ourselves be truly happy because to us happiness usually meant that something heartbreaking was just around the corner. I remember a time when I was newly married and laying in my husband's arms and thinking how happy I was. Then I just started crying uncontrollably. I felt like because I was so happy, I was going to lose it all. I was going to lose him.

My whole family had this crippling fear of happiness. It sounds silly, I know. Who would not want to be happy? And we did—we wanted happiness so very badly. But to us, happiness came with a price. For with happiness came sorrow.

My brother and I were so young when our mom got sick. Our brains were still developing. The trauma, the fear, the unknown, was what our lives were mostly made of. It's what trained our brains. The trauma built an alarm system within us, so whenever we felt hurt, when we felt a feeling that was similar to what we felt as a child, we were triggered. We would cry, scream, panic, and our bodies would freeze, terrified to relive the nightmare that our childhoods often were. Being raised during a time of trauma trained us never to trust happiness and that people you love the most leave. This alarm kept us sharp, awake, and on high alert from any threat. Our minds, bodies, and souls had been through enough; the alarm was an attempt to keep us safe. But over time, it was clear it was holding us back. It was hindering our ability to trust and to receive love. It kept our minds constantly racing, with our minds filled with fear, there was little room for peace. The alarm no longer kept us safe, but it kept us from being our best selves. To overcome what had been programmed into our brains was hard. It takes real effort and hard work to train your brain what is true and to focus on the present and not the past. We were constantly living in fear, fear of the past and of experiencing anything similar to it. Daily I fight to direct my mind and my heart to the truth. I remind myself that not everyone I love will leave, to accept that I do not know what the future holds or have any control over other people's actions, to love even in the unknown, that happiness doesn't always end in tragedy, and that good things can just be good. I write these words now not fully having it all figured out; my alarm still sounds, my fears that are generated from my past still fill my mind, but all I can do is remind myself of the truth and continue the work till the day my mind will just know that I have nothing to fear.

Without the safety net, without the alarm trying to save us, maybe we could finally enjoy the great things in life. Like the birth of a beautiful baby or meeting the love of your life—or even just simple things like a family member's birthday or a date night with a spouse or partner. We are still learning to let go and just live. No matter how hard we try, we will never truly forget the past. We just can't let ourselves get stuck in it. We need to look at what is ahead, and we have to make the choice each day to refuse to let fear rule over us. After a great loss, there is emptiness and a void in the shape of the person you lost. I have fought my entire life. I have fought against lies, sadness, pain, people, and death, and it has left me broken and exhausted. I have never stopped fighting. Fighting is not a bad thing, but sometimes we just need to take a minute, breathe, and just be still.

We lived twelve long years fighting sickness and disease. We battled against depression and pain. The odds often seemed stacked against us. Our lives were filled with hospitals, fear, grief, cancer, tears—it seemed never-ending. That life was certainly difficult, and at times, it seemed impossible to continue, but that was the life we knew. It became familiar and strangely comfortable. When my mother passed away, the life we had always known vanished. Life may have been hard, but the truth was we felt like we would rather live with the pain than live without our mom and my dad without his wife.

A few years ago, my dad and I went out for dinner just the two of us. We talked about our lives and reminisced about Mom like we often do. We talked about the good times and the bad. After a moment of silence, I looked at him and asked, "If you could do it all over again, knowing how it would turn out, would you? If you could go back in time, would you still marry mom knowing all that you know now?"

Without pause, he answered, "In a heartbeat."

My dad retired six months before Mom's passing. He did this to be able to spend more time at home with her. For him, everything he did was for her. She was so much of who we were. With her gone, there was more than a void in all of our lives and hearts.

We felt more lost than we ever had before. What were we supposed to do now? We spent so much of our time with our mom. Most of our thoughts and prayers were about her. With her gone, we no longer knew what to do with ourselves. It felt like we were starting a whole new life. On one hand, we were scared to death. A life without our mom seemed like no life at all. How could we live without her? But, on the other hand, it was a fresh start, a clean slate. It was time to move on and start to heal, no matter how impossible that seemed.

After my mom died, things were so quiet. My whole life before she died had been nothing but chaos. It was normal, and it was all I knew. And it was so strange suddenly living with everything so still and quiet. You'd think it would make me want to fill the quiet with something, but it didn't. Songs started to seem meaningless to me. When I would open my mouth to sing, nothing would come out. So much of her voice is in mine, and it pained me too much to hear it. My sadness was so strong that I lost the one thing that made me feel close to my mother. But as time has passed, my wounds have started to heal. Now, every time I open up my mouth to sing, I sing as loud as I can, and I think of her.

My husband's aunt once told me a story. She and her husband were on vacation. A guy approached them, and they were mugged;

he took everything they had on them. After it happened, they rushed to their hotel, scared and shaken up. An hour later, she looked down and noticed a gash in her arm and blood dripping onto the floor. She had been cut by the mugger and didn't even know. She didn't feel any pain at all because she was too consumed with what had just happened.

When you are injured or in great pain, adrenaline plays a huge role. When you have been in an accident or through a great trauma of some sort, adrenaline starts pumping through your veins. Sometimes the adrenaline is so strong you don't feel tired when you are exhausted, or you don't feel pain when you are hurt; sometimes injuries can even go undetected because the adrenaline is keeping you so alert. You may not even know how extensive your injuries are until it is too late. As soon as that all wears off and as soon as your body rests, everything that was hiding under all that adrenaline catches up with you and you fully succumb to the injuries and pain that was there all along. In a way, that is what it was like for us after my mother died. When she was alive, we were so wrapped up in her and what she needed, we didn't have time to worry about our own pain. When you are in the midst of tragedy, it is quite difficult to deal with the pain. Things for us were always moving so fast; life was filled with so many things to deal with, we never had time to stop and think about how it was affecting us and what it was doing to us. We never really knew how badly our situation was affecting us. We weren't even aware of how wounded we really were. Everyone around us could see it, but we couldn't always. When my mother passed, the pain flooded us, and we were completely overwhelmed. With everything quiet and still, we were forced to confront our pain and everything we had been through. In the silence, all we could hear were the screams of our pain and no matter how hard we tried, we could not ignore it. We were left with wounds we never knew we had and pain that was catastrophic. But now that we are able to really feel them, our wounds are finally healing.

—

So often the reality of how unfair this all was just hits us. We started to notice all the stuff we were missing and all the stuff our mother was missing. It started to become hard to watch other people's relationships with their mothers. It often just reminded me of what I didn't have. One day I was at a friend's house and she was cooking a meal for her family. She forgot a step in her recipe, so she picked up the phone and called her mom, who walked her step by step through the recipe. As my friend was on the phone with her mom, tears streamed down my face. How I longed to call my mother, to ask her life's simple questions, to just hear her voice.

I feel my mother's absence every day of my life. And so does the rest of my family. She is missing everything. She will never know my children or see the woman I have become. She won't get to grow old with my dad, like they were supposed to. This was not how life was supposed to be. It just isn't fair. It's not fair that Matthew, Brian, and I have to live life without our mom, and my dad has to go on without his wife. It's not fair that my kids will never experience the beauty of their grandmother.

It is okay to feel robbed and hurt. It is okay to miss the ones I have lost. It's when I choose to live in a place of despair, where things can get dark. Every day I have to choose to pick myself up and move forward. Even if at times I have to crawl, that's okay, I just have to keep moving. If I don't, the pain and anger I feel will flow over into my other relationships. I will start to expect them to fill the void and give me everything I am lacking, and that's an unfair expectation. Going through what I did taught me that no matter what lies ahead, I can face it. If I have to walk through the fire again, I know that I will make it through the other side. Pain will never be easy, and it may leave scars, but those scars tell a story, a story that I will forever be grateful for.

⁓

My mom's birthday and the anniversary of her death fall on or near Thanksgiving each year. So, on every Thanksgiving, I don't feel very thankful—instead I grieve and long for what I no longer have.

Holidays after a loved one has passed are brutal and cruel. They so blatantly remind you of what you are missing in your life. Every Christmas, Thanksgiving, Mother's Day, and Easter are not the same without them there.

Mother's Day is the worst for me. It saddens me having to watch everyone else celebrate their mothers when I no longer have mine. But feeling this way on every holiday was making me bitter and ungrateful, and the state of my heart was not good at all, and that made it harder to move forward.

Thanksgiving has just come and gone, but this time, things were different. This time I chose to be thankful. I am thankful I got to know her at all. I am glad I got to have her as my mother even if it was just for a little while. I am so very thankful for the family and friends I do have. I also started being thankful for the hard times, even for the ones I have not yet experienced. Because they have made me who I am today, and they will continue to shape me into who I am meant to be.

Going on without your loved one is painful. The other night all the pain that was within me overflowed, and I began to sob. For hours I cried, and I just kept thinking, "I miss my mom. I miss my mom. Why did she have to leave me?" I used to think that when I would break down over my past and the loss of my mom, it would mean I was not healed. But I am realizing that just because I cry, it doesn't mean I am not healed; it just means I am human. It is possible to feel sadness and loss and still be whole. The sadness I have for my mom no longer being here with me is something I will probably carry forever. My grief is just evidence of the love I had for my mother.

———

Healing for my family was not easy, and even though many years have passed, our healing is still not complete. For some of us, healing felt like we had to let Mom go, and letting go meant forgetting, and we did not want to do that. So, every time we tried to heal, resistance met us and hindered our progress. But eventually, healing caught up with us. The pain became too great to carry, and we could no longer resist. We would often fight the tears, but now we just let them wash us clean. Healing is messy. It is far from easy. But God never promised it would be easy. He just promised we would never have to walk it alone.

The pain we have experienced is rooted deep within us, and there are things we can't ever forget or escape. Simple things remind us of our pain and daily we have to work through our past. We can't erase what happened or undo it. But we do have a choice: we can let it rule us and cripple us, or we can let it shape us and teach us.

Letters to You

To Mommy,

I would be lying if I said life without you is easy. I feel your absence in every moment of my life. I will never stop missing you and wishing you were here holding me. When I was in labor with my second child, I looked at James with a tear streaming down my face and said, "I wish my mommy was here." And every day I wish for that. I wish you could be here. I need you here and some days it kills me that you are not. I wish you could take me shopping and give me advice I often desperately need. I wish you could hold your grandbabies, and I wish that they could know you and all your beauty. Even though they will never meet you, I will tell them your story. I will tell them of your strength, and I will tell them of your joy and great faith. You may be gone, but I promise that what you have done on this earth will never be forgotten. I surely will never forget you. You impacted my life in every way, and you left an imprint on my heart. I am who I am because of you. Even though we are worlds apart, I know you are not that far. I hear you when I sing. I meet you in my dreams. I see you in my daughter's smile, and I see your joy when my son laughs. Even though you are gone, you are all around me. Dad often tells me that I am just like you, which is the highest compliment I have ever received. You are someone I admire the most, and I daily pray that I would have your strength and faith. Even if just a tiny part of you lives in me, I would be blessed.

I have found a man who makes me happy; he protects me and loves me like I always longed to be. You never really got to know James, but I know you would love him. Thank you for the amazing example you and dad set for me. Growing up I watched your amazing love story, and I hoped I would have a love like that one day. And now I do. I just pray we can be the great example to our kids like you were to us. I love you, Mommy. I love you so much it hurts. I miss you every day. I miss your motherly touch and your friendship. My life is not the same without you in it. But when I feel really low and I am missing you so bad, I close my eyes and I picture you *walking in the most beautiful place. You are whole and you are happy; your joy is restored and you are running free. And clutched in your hand is the hand of glory. I know that you are where you belong. It is where you have always belonged. You are forever in my heart and for the rest of my life I will keep you close.*

I love you, Mommy.
Your daughter,
Maralee
(written 2011)

Hey Mom,
Remember when we went to Disneyland? Maralee and Dad went off on their own and me and you went off on ours. We had so much fun, and it was the only real memory I have of us hanging out together, and it was a good one. Remember when I tricked you into going on that roller coaster? I said it wasn't fast, but man was it fast, and you screamed so loud, but I think you had fun on it even though you didn't say it. I will always remember that day and cherish that memory for as long as I live.

If you were right in front of me, I wouldn't say anything at first. I would grab you and hug you very tightly and then tell you I wish I got to know you better and that I love you.

Love,
Matthew
(written 2011)

Kathy,
If you were here right now, I would tell you that you were the best thing that ever happened to me, and that I would do it all over again.

Even So

I love you, Kathy, and I thank Jesus He made us soul mates and that we have a date in Heaven.

I really miss you and I wish you were here.

Love,
Chris
(written 2011)

CHAPTER FOURTEEN

Holding Both

So in the end every major disaster, every
tiny error, every wrong turning,
every fragment of discarded clay, all the blood,
sweat and tears - everything has meaning.
I give it meaning. I reuse, reshape, recast all that goes wrong
so that in the end nothing is wasted and
nothing is without significance
and nothing ceases to be precious to me.
~ Harriet March as quoted by Susan Howatch
in Rob Bell's "Drops like Stars"

I have spent some time learning about how my brain works to better understand myself and why I react the way that I do. At a young age, my life's narrative started to form. There was a story I would make up about myself based on words said to me and the things happening to me and around me. My developing brain relied on the information it was given from circumstances and surroundings. My brain would piece together all the information like a puzzle and would dictate how I viewed myself and the world. It would tell me what was safe and what wasn't. It often did its best to protect me and sometimes that meant rewriting my memories and blocking certain things out.

147

Many negative and traumatizing things happened to me while my brain was still forming, so my brain was programmed to believe that what was happening around me was how the world really was. It perceived it as normal. As I grew and my circumstances changed, my brain still continued to operate on the previous data it had been given. During my childhood and teen years, not much felt safe or secure and as I matured and things for me improved, anything that felt familiar I still saw as a threat and a danger. I saw things the same way I did when things were much worse. My brain was programmed to be on high alert at all times and I didn't know how to turn it off. I saw things so differently than the others around me. Every slight was wounding, every loud noise was frightening. Upsetting things would traumatize me, change rattled me, every mean word had me doubting myself and questioning my identity. I kept following the same patterns and I kept believing what my brain said was true. For a very long time, I never questioned it. I never considered that things weren't actually how I saw them. I reached a point where I knew I had to change the way my brain saw the world and how it processed danger and trauma. But first, I had to identify what major things contributed to my way of thinking in the first place.

"I love your mom more than you," my dad uttered to me with such anger and sadness. We were sitting in the hospital waiting room. It was a large, beige room with the most uncomfortable chairs. The waiting area was located on the lowest level of the hospital. It was always busy. People were constantly walking briskly from one end to the other. I don't quite remember what prompted my dad to say this to me. My guess is I was seeking more of his attention or perhaps it was in response to me sharing my disdain for his constant absence. No matter the reason, that statement hurt me. I do not remember my response. I just remember being shocked. I remember tears and slouching down in that terrible chair. I remember how he was sitting, legs crossed and hands on his lap. I remember the expression on his face. He looked annoyed and had tear-filled eyes. She was his wife. Maybe that's how it was supposed to be. I questioned the idea, trying my best to rationalize and make sense of it. As I grew older and got married and had children of my own, I started to explore this further. I thought, "Now I can understand where he was coming from." But I could never fully understand my dad's words. I love my husband and I love my kids. But I love them both very differently. I am not sure I could say I love one more than another. No matter if what he said was true or right or not, it cut me. In that moment, something shifted in my brain. It added to the narrative that I was not loved or important.

"If your mom dies, I want to take a gun and put a bullet in my head." My brother, my dad, and I were at Boston Pizza for lunch. My dad was extremely sad. My mom was going through one of her sicker times. We were having lunch, just us three, to talk things through, figure out what to do, and where to go from there. I am not sure when during the meal this slipped out or what made him say it. I think our conversation started to drift toward the topic of her dying, a possibility that was constantly hovering over us. Matthew and I sat stunned. We pleaded for him not to talk that way.

We became incredibly emotional and afraid. We knew how sincere that statement was. It wasn't just a flippant remark. He really meant it. This was the first time we heard such a comment from him, but it certainly wasn't the last. We tried desperately to convince him that we needed him with us and that we couldn't handle him leaving us. For days, years really, Matthew and I wrestled with his words. Why would he want to leave us? Do we not matter? He can't live without his wife, but he can leave us behind? Most days reaffirmed the story I was telling myself.

All the comments my mom made to me changed me forever. Words of "I hate you" were hurled at me, served alongside some physical abuse. Yes, she was sick. Yes, I think the tumors made her do it. But that fact changes nothing. It still affected me and how I saw myself. I needed a loving mother and that is not always what I got. Her actions toward me fanned the flame of my insecurities, and my self-worth took a huge beating. I started to struggle with this haunting and terrifying question: if my own mother didn't love me, then is there anything about me worth loving? And for a while, I truly believed the answer to that question was no.

That bully from kindergarten I talked about in the beginning of the book also added to my story. It may be the first memory I have where I entertained the thought that I wasn't enough.

My parents loved me and my brother, I know this for sure. I think I always knew it. What I also know was that no matter how much they loved us and how much they wished they could pour it out on us, they got to a place where they were unable to actually show and give us that love. There was no time or energy for it. We were loved but the love never really could reach us. It often got caught up in the chaos. There were moments where it broke free and made its way to my brother and me. But for a long time, we basically lived with very little and definitely not enough. We knew there was love but we didn't always have the evidence of it. We just had to believe it was there and rely on past memories to prove it really did exist.

All the abuse I faced in my childhood and teen years told me everything I needed to know about myself. I faced many different forms of abuse by many different people, but it all carried the same message. It told me that I was unimportant, that I didn't matter, that I was completely expendable, and that nothing about me was good enough. And when the abuse told me who I was, I believed it. I rationalized it because from my perspective you don't treat something of value with such disregard. Every decision stemmed from this belief. Every relationship was based on what the abuse told me to be true.

I worked very hard in every relationship I had to prove to them how valuable and irreplaceable I was, which made for many one-sided relationships and made room for even more abuse. But now as I get older, the old narrative is starting to fall apart, and I am starting to see the holes in it. I have started to see the lies and I am starting to believe the truth. I now see that the way others treated me is not proof that I was not enough, but just maybe it is proof that they did not believe that they were.

As time went on in my mother's illness, my self-narrative got more and more destructive and distorted. The story that I was unloved and unimportant got fueled by my surroundings and circumstances. Throughout my childhood, my brain was conditioned to think my needs and emotions were not important. Every time something came up for me, something bigger came up for my mom. My brother and I were both constantly being lost in the shuffle. If an overwhelming situation came up and something had to give in our family, it would be me and Matthew who would have to bend and sacrifice. Our needs were just not as great as my mom's. We learned to adapt, learned how to survive. We fixed our problems ourselves, or we shoved our emotions down or let them out in places and in situations that were not appropriate.

Home is supposed to be a safe place but for me it wasn't. People say that kids act out more at home than they do in public because they feel safer at home. They trust the people in their home to see who they really are. They feel safe enough to be real; they don't feel the need to pretend. They feel they have the freedom to struggle and be tired. It's difficult for children to be on their best behaviour all day at school. It wears on them and for kids it takes great effort. So when they get home, they often let it all out.

For me, there was no room for my meltdowns, panics, drama, or my pain; our home was already at capacity. So I made the outside my safe place, although it wasn't safe at all. When out with friends, I would panic and let all I was holding in come out. It took all my effort to somewhat hold it together inside the walls of my home, so when I would leave them, things got messy. It took all my strength to be the best daughter I could, to not make any more waves than there already was. I tried my best to hold it together inside the house, so when I would leave, I would often fall apart.

I beat myself up for so long for how I would act in public. I was embarrassed and ashamed. But as I explored this in therapy, I discovered why I did it. There is always a why behind the struggle. A lot of the people I was with could not see the why and some didn't really care to ask. It also helped me to look at other people's struggles differently too. Now when I am taken aback by someone's behaviour, I look for the why; I look for the reason. Discovering my own why (which I didn't know until twelve years later) gave me so much freedom. It released me from my shame. The why gave me grace.

I wasn't a bad person or lacking in self-control; I wasn't weak or a drama queen. I was hurting, I was sad, I wanted to know that I was loved and that I mattered.

The relationship with my parents was and is complicated. They are as great and wonderful as I say, but there is also so much hurt there. I truly believe their character rings truer and louder than their flaws and mistakes but still this relationship has made for some murky waters. It has made it incredibly hard to see through. Humans are imperfect. We are good and we are flawed. And when it comes to my family's story, I have to make space for both, for all of it. The inspiring, the awful, the noble and the regrettable. There are lessons in the flaws and errors. The bad sometimes fuels the good. The ugliness can make the beautiful more stunning. I try hard to make space for both, as both of them have led me to where I stand now and contributed to who I am.

Honouring it all can be strange and awkward. It can be a confusing process, as my thoughts and feelings can be contradictory, but it is all the truth. I didn't have the strength before to feel both at once. I would alternate from one to the other. Holding them both helps me respect what I have been through. It grants me time to grieve and to heal. Holding both throws out the rule book. I can be grateful for what I have and grieve for what I have lost at the same time. I can love and be disappointed. I can heal and I can be happy, I can be full of fear and full of courage. It is all valuable and it all matters. In order to change my thinking, the way my brain sees things, I need to change the way I talk to and about myself. It means living a wholehearted life, which for me means engaging every part of myself and operating from a place where I know that I am enough, even when I don't always believe it. In order to engage my whole heart, I have to accept the heartache too. I need to use everything that is given to me. I will waste nothing.

CHAPTER FIFTEEN

The Art of Holding On and Letting Go

What you lost in the fire, you can find in the ashes.
~ The Magnificent 7 (movie)

For Christmas one year my husband surprised me when he handed me a beautiful gold box. Bursting with excitement I quickly opened my present. As I slowly lifted the top, I saw a silver necklace. As I lifted the beautiful delicate silver chain from the box, I noticed words hanging from it that read, "Don't let go." He then told me he had a lady copy those words in my mother's handwriting. I held the necklace in my hand and sobbed. It was the most beautiful present I have ever been given. With tears still lingering in my eyes, I stared at the necklace and as I did, I began to think about the words on the necklace, and what the words "Don't let go" meant to me. I have always struggled, more now than ever, with knowing when to hold on tight and when to let go. I thought of all the things the term "letting go" can mean or represent. It can mean getting rid of what hurts or offends you, it can be choosing to no longer hold onto the past, it can also be saying goodbye to someone you love. Another way to let go can be giving up and choosing to no longer hold onto hope.

The concept of holding on and letting go can be a bit confusing. Sometimes we hold on to things we shouldn't and let go of the things we should have held close. It can be a bit overwhelming, and at times, I honestly don't know when to do either.

Letting go can be difficult because there are some things that you don't want to let go of, no matter how much those things may hurt. For me, pain became comfortable, it was my normal. And to let go of the only thing I've ever truly known was no easy thing. No matter how much I was hurting, it didn't change the fact that moving forward was terrifying. Everything I had experienced, good or bad, all became a part of who I was. Letting go meant healing. Who would I be if I wasn't broken? When you let go, when you walk away from what is hurting, you don't know what you will find on the other side. For all you know, you could just find more pain. There were also some things I had to let go of concerning my mom. Although I do everything I can to honour my mother's memory, and I respect her life and her story and I hold her up high on a pedestal, there is another side of it all.

The relationship between me and my mom is so complicated. Through my life, I loved and honoured her, but in the same breath, I was so angry and wounded by her. Every scream from her mouth to my ears, every seizure, every hospital admittance, ever hurtful word she said but never meant, every hit, every slap left its mark. So, I often wrestle with conflicting feelings. I respect my mom's story; she really was the woman I describe, but her journey, the effects of her sickness, has set my life on a path that has often ripped me apart. While our journey left me stronger, it also left so many scars.

The hurt I hold is heavy. I've been wounded and pushed down, and one of the people who hurt me the most is my mother. Over my life, I have seen things I wish I hadn't and been through things I can't forget. Although I may not forget, I can forgive. Forgiveness is the ultimate way to let go. It is the best way to find healing and freedom. Not for them, but for you. And the best part of letting go of anger, hurt, and resentment is that it leaves room for love. I had to acknowledge and accept what my mom put me through and then set it free. I loosened my grip on all the unkind words my mom spoke to me and hurtful actions she did toward me and, as I did, those things lost their grip on me. Letting go, no longer holding tightly to the past, left more room to miss her and love her. I choose to accept and then let go, so I can firmly hold onto my mom and to all her life has to teach me.

This world is full of people who may mistreat you, judge you, and speak unkindly, and I have had my share of all those. I have noticed that after I have been hurt, I become more cautious around people, and I become scared the past may repeat itself. Although being cautious can be a good thing, in my case, it was stopping me from being close and having relationships with others. Forgiveness gave me the chance to overcome my fear of being hurt and helped connect me with people I could rely on. Forgiveness gives you the freedom to make connections.

I think there is a big misconception about letting go—that it is an easy process. That all you have to do to get rid of what's ailing you is to no longer care about it, to choose not to think about it, to choose to no longer let it bug you—and problem solved. If it was just as easy as making a simple choice, then I would have done it long ago. Letting go is hard work. Nothing in this life comes easy, especially the things worth obtaining. So often when I'm dealing with my pain, I hear people advise, "You've just got to let it go." But those words feel so empty. Those words often leave me with so many questions, mostly "How do I do it?" I have learned that letting go is not something you just do once; it's something you have to keep doing every day. It has to be a daily conscious choice. Letting go requires awareness and being intentional with your thoughts and actions. In my life, things creep up on me on a daily basis—things I never expected to bug me. Hurt, shame, fear, regret, and resentment are just a few of the things that often show their ugly face to me, and usually when I least expect it. And each time those things make an appearance, I have to make the active choice to let it go. I wish

I could just choose to no longer feel any of those things, but alas, it's not that simple. When those feelings come upon me, when an unkind word is spoken to me, and I am transported back in time to my past—where for a second I become that hurt, broken girl I used to be—I choose to bring myself back. I remind myself of who I know I am. I remind myself that no word can change my heart, and I let it all go. Letting something go doesn't mean it won't come back. For me sometimes the very thing I chose to get rid of turns up again moments later. But I will keep making the choice as long as it takes.

As I wear that beautiful necklace around my neck, I am reminded of what things I should hold on tight to.

Faith is the most important one to me. It has been a constant in my life. Faith has been the foundation of my entire life. It was what my life was built on. There have been many times when I didn't understand why my life was the way it was. Why was my mom so sick? Why was my dad so sad? Why was life so hard? And all of those whys made me want to let go, they made me want to run and never look back, they made me want to push Him away, and to be honest, sometimes I did. I am thankful because if I wasn't tethered to something bigger than myself, I would have fallen off the edge. Believing in God meant my hands were never empty; it meant I was never truly alone; it meant hope. On days where I felt like I didn't have much of anything, a little bit of hope seemed like more than enough. Holding onto Him helps me to hold onto life and to let go of all the things I don't need. In my world, there were times when peace would vanish, when peace would seem but a myth, in Him I could find it. With Him I could catch my breath.

Family. My past holds a lot of hurt for me and for my dad and brothers. We have caused each other a lot of heartache and pain over the years. Even though we all love each other very much we weren't always kind to one another. Through all of the sickness and pain, we had often felt unloved and forgotten. So once in a while, all those memories of feeling unloved and forgotten sneak up on me, and I feel like I did all those years ago. But the thing is, if I hold on to those feelings, my relationship with my family would change. If I didn't forgive them, I may not have them at all.

I have been through so much with them. We've seen the good times, the bad times, and the even worse times. We have had our fights and disagreements, and despite all we have endured, they are still among the people that mean the most to me. The pain and hurt that built up in our hearts over the years from things said and done started to put a strain on our relationships and our hearts. My family may drive me insane at times, and vice versa I'm sure, but they are the only ones who really know what I have been through because they went through it right along with me. They understand my heartbreak over losing Mom, and they get the struggle of living without her. Having them in my life is instrumental to moving on and finding healing. Talking to someone who truly "gets it" is no small thing. Having support is huge; it keeps you from going through it all on your own. So no matter what they have done, no matter the bitterness or the resentment, I choose to forgive and let go. I am starting to learn that sometimes you have to let go so you can hold on.

My Husband. Over the years, I have faced a lot of rejection, have dealt with emotional abuse from others, and have heard the most hurtful words, and I carried those words with me for years. When I met James, I was a broken shell of a person. I had been through the ringer and it showed. When we started dating, every day I expected him to break up with me, and after the end of each day, I was extremely surprised when he didn't. There were times I was so sure he would end things with me, I would try to break up with him. I thought that I could do the rejecting and save myself the humiliation. James never allowed that. Others would see my broken soul and my destructive behaviors and go running for the hills, but James saw me—he saw through my brokenness and insecurities and he did run but not away from me, but toward me. Nothing made him leave, even when he had good reason to; he stayed. But with all of that assurance, I still had a hard time trusting him. This is a perfect example of letting go in a negative way. I tried to let go when I should have held on. Thankfully, James held on tight enough for both of us. I felt so undeserving of anything good, and I often tried to sabotage everything. I carried my hurts from past relationships, from my parents, from friends into our marriage. My past was so blinding I was unable to see clearly. In a marriage, you fight, you have disagreements, but I was so fearful of losing his love that anything slightly negative from him sent me into major panic attacks. Panic attacks so bad, I would black out for a minute. Attacks so bad, I lost control. I would scream and throw things, I would kick and throw my body around. I felt like the fear and agony would kill me and at times I wished that it would. I could not handle even the thought of being unloved—especially from him. The fear of being left or not loved enough was so terrifying that I felt physically unsafe and my body often went into a fight or flight response. No matter how often James would show his love for me and prove that he wouldn't leave and tell me I could not lose his love, I still questioned it, no matter how much I tried I couldn't trust it. A thought I would have was, "In my life, nothing good ever lasted long, so why would it start now?" Happiness was not something I was used to, and therefore, I didn't trust it. I used to and sometimes still do take my pain out on James. The saying "You hurt the ones you love" rings too true for me. My intense love for James often fanned my profound fear. We established earlier that my underlying struggle and the story that I made up for myself and convinced myself was truth was that I am not loved or important. So because he was the one I loved, most of my reactions were defensive even if he hadn't really done anything. I was easily triggered by him because I was easily shaken. I was always on high alert.

Not being able to let go of all my past hurts and fears stopped me from truly loving James and letting him truly love me. I had mentioned earlier letting go leaves room for you to give love, but it also leaves room to receive it. All the stuff I was holding on to created a barrier between James and me, so he could never truly reach me or I him. I came across another saying the other day. It read, *If you don't heal what hurt you, you'll bleed on people who didn't cut you.* This is exactly what was happening in my marriage. James wasn't the one who hurt me, yet he was the one I was punishing. My past was not his fault, yet he was paying the price. Over the last few years, I have worked very hard at "letting go" so I could really hold onto my beloved husband. I had to get more deliberate with my reactions and more aware of my reason behind my actions. As I found healing, I found a love so true and good. For each hurt, rejection, and unloved feeling that would disappear, we were able to take a step toward each other.

Friends. There is nothing quite like a friend—someone to talk with, laugh and cry with. Although James is my best friend, there are some things that men just don't understand and that they probably don't want to. There is something about having someone who can truly relate to your situation, whether it is minor or major. There is something special about sharing a cup of coffee and chatting while you watch your children play, getting out of the house for a movie or calling for a helping hand when you need it. There were times when I have had this kind of support and there were times when I haven't. And the times when I haven't were some of the hardest and loneliest times of my life.

Now, friends are only human, which means they are imperfect and make mistakes, which unfortunately can also mean you may get hurt. I have had friends flat-out reject me, and I have had friends drift away from me slowly. Losing friends is not easy, and I would often let that affect how I viewed myself. I would take my past rejections from friends as proof that I am not enough. I didn't want to get any more hurt than I already was. I was not sure my heart could take anymore. The safest bet seemed to be loneliness. While loneliness stopped me from being hurt, loneliness also stopped me from being loved. Rejection from others had me second-guessing every word I spoke, every action, everything I was and did, afraid that I might offend and be discarded. I had stopped being true to myself in fear that I was the reason I was so often alone.

During my mother's illness, my closest friends helped me through the darkest days. Meals were prepared and brought to the hospital. Ears were lent as I would vent and yell over things that upset and burdened me. Shoulders were offered when I needed a place to cry. And tears were shared when I was at my saddest. When my mother died, one of my closest friends flew to B.C. from Ontario just to support me and help with my newborn. I didn't even have to ask; she just showed up. The night after we buried my mom, my girlfriends threw me a spa night. They cuddled my sweet baby boy as they took turns pampering me and helping me relax. They gave me a facial, manicure, and pedicure, while we all talked and laughed. After the week I had been through, I truly needed a laugh—not just any laugh but one of those laughs that come from the depths of your belly, the ones where you can't catch your breath, you're laughing so hard. Laughter has a way of changing things and lifting your spirit. Friendship is the best way to get that kind of laughter. Friendship can be grueling and hard. But it can also be rewarding and uplifting. There is beauty in having people in your corner cheering you on. There is something beautiful about a friend.

Life can be a daily struggle with all the responsibilities and all the unexpected things that are thrown our way on top of dealing with our past and what is inside our hearts. It can sometimes be unbearable. The life of a wife and a mother can be wonderful but, at times, daunting. It is full of sleepless nights, full of crying babies, kids screaming throughout the day, children awaking from bad dreams, and sickness plaguing your house at the worst possible times. You seem to fall asleep just as it's time to wake up. You've got to make breakfasts, make lunches, chauffeur your family around, clean the house, grocery shop, plan supper, make supper, and so much more—meanwhile, there is a pile of laundry that never seems to shrink no matter how many loads you do. And in the midst of all that, you have hurts and fears stirring in your heart and the past that you tried to leave behind keeps catching up to you. Things pop up throughout your day that act as a painful reminder of the trauma and agony that you once had to endure. But you can't wallow in it or truly feel it because your list is already too long and there is just no room for anything else. But because each day demands so much of you, you push your heartaches and the pain of your past deeper and deeper down. You ignore the things nagging at your soul because there doesn't seem room for any personal things. But the more you ignore your feelings, the bigger the pile gets until the pain has nowhere to go, and it all just gets to be too much.

For my husband, it can often be the same kind of thing. He works hard all day, comes home, and helps with the kids, helps with baths and bedtime. And when the day is done, there is seldom a minute for himself. Although our family is worth the sacrifices, it can be hard. Sometimes the burden of life weighs too heavily, and the load is more than we can bear, and at times, it may feel like the only way out is to choose the negative side of letting go and giving up. There have been many days when I have felt like this, many days where I have been so overwhelmed that I would just weep into my giant pile of laundry. It's hard to work out your issues when you can't even find the time to take a shower.

I often look around at other women who seem perfectly put together, while I have one eye lined and food in my hair. There are women who seem like they are breezing through life, while I fight through most of mine. The pain in my heart is often heavy and my self-doubt consumes me. There are times where I feel incredibly tired and worn—not just physically but deep within my bones. Some days, lies fill my head; they fill it so full there is no room for hope, only despair, and for a while, everything that is good drowns in it. And my mind is tricked into thinking there is only one way out. I let suicide be an option many years ago, and ever since it's been knocking at my door. And daily I fight hard not to let it in. The years seem to just keep passing me by and there are days I feel like complete healing may never come, like my tears may never dry.

There are nights where I hide in the bathroom and cry, sobbing for what I have lost and what I will never have. I let it all out. I wipe my tears and take big breaths in and out. I struggle to stand, but find my footing, stumble into bed, and fall asleep. I awake in the morning and keep on fighting. I don't believe life for me will ever be "breezy", but maybe that's okay because being a fighter keeps me strong. Sometimes I feel like I should be all better by now, that there should be no more tears. I once read something on Facebook: "When you no longer cry when you tell your story you know that healing has come." It sounds beautiful, but I don't think that is true. There is so much advice out there trying to tell you when you'll know you're healed and all better. But the truth is there is no gauge; sometimes when I tell my story, even as I write these words tears show up—not every time but sometimes. Crying when you think about your past doesn't mean you're not moving on or that you are not healed. Be raw and honest. Let your authenticity show. Maybe just telling your story at all means you're closer to healing than you think. Maybe the fact that you fall apart and then pick yourself up shows how far you've come from where you were. There is no right way to grieve, no right way to work through your issues. I will always cry over my mom and my past. The tears may be fewer, but I welcome them when they come. They don't mean failure. It doesn't set me back. They mean love. Crying gives me an outlet; it makes room for the many other things I have yet to face. I have asked, "When will I be finished? When will the healing be done?" And maybe the answer is never. I used to find that thought depressing, but now I find it comforting. There is no deadline; there is no rush, no pressure. This allows me to really feel. It allows me to not hold myself back. I'm starting to find the beauty in imperfection, the opportunities that are discovered through my pain and the cleansing my tears provide. I used to be so embarrassed that I'm not done healing yet. I used to think that made me weak, but I am discovering that it makes me strong. Still being in the midst gives me more opportunities than if I were done. I once got into a habit of ignoring my pain. Now I have learned to embrace it in all its ugliness. I have discovered the more I let myself feel, the more happiness I discover, and the closer I get to feeling free. But the more I suppress myself, the more of a prisoner I become. I thought ignoring it would cure me, but it would have killed me. Healing is a process, and with each step, life gets brighter and the darkness, more dim.

My husband found those words that hang around my neck in my mother's letters. Those words were discovered in the middle of a prayer where she called out to God, "Hold me close and don't let go." "Don't let go" has now become my prayer to God and an encouragement to keep moving onward. If you have the unbearable urge to give up and let go, then let go of the pain that binds you, the past that haunts you, and the burdens that keep pushing you down.

May you never give up, may you hold onto hope, may you hold onto peace, and may you let go of all that weighs you down. May you find freedom in the art of holding on and letting go.

FINAL THOUGHTS

The shadow proves the sunshine.
~ Switchfoot

My life has not always been easy. My past has had rough edges that often cut me deeply. There has been a flood of disappointments and heartache. I have lost a mother who I will miss and cry over for the rest of my life. I have been wounded and knocked down. I have seen darkness, and I have known pain.

But as I opened my mouth and started sharing my story, as I let the pen release what I had been holding back for so long, as I let people see the ugly so it could be made beautiful, healing came. The sun came. I started out in the darkest forest where the road was narrow and the nights were cold. But now I see the clearing, the sun shining through the trees. And after many years, I am finally making my way out the other side. I can say I have seen the rain, but now I can also say I have seen the sun.

May your journey through the forest strengthen you, may you share your story, for it's a story that is worth being told, and may it set you free. May you find the peace you long for, the hope you need, the love you deserve, and the healing that you strive for. And may you find beauty in the darkness.

You make beautiful things; You make
beautiful things out of the dust
You make beautiful things You make beautiful things out of us
~ Gungor

THANK YOU

Without **You** I would have no hope, no light, and no peace. In **You** I found my worth and my place. The mere act of believing in **You** and loving **You** has changed me and saved my life.

To my mother, no matter how things ended up, I am so grateful that you were my mom. I am blessed I got to see your faith and heart up close. Thank you for the beautiful example you have set for me and my family. Thank you for teaching me to never give up, for teaching me that it's not how you start but how you finish. And you finished well, Mommy. Your mere presence in my life has changed me forever. I am just so honoured that I got to be part of your story—one I will tell until my final breath.

To my beloved husband, you saved me in more ways than I could ever express. Thank you for all your support and all your love. Thank you for cheering me on every step of the way. Thank you for always seeing me. Thank you for always believing in me when others didn't. I could not have done this without you. I love you with all my heart.

To my beautiful children, you inspire me daily and constantly bless my heart. You three are the most amazing humans, you are valuable, and you are loved, deeply and completely. I am so completely grateful that you are my kids and that I get to walk along side you in your journeys. I find my joy in being your mom.

To my dad, thank you for not just supporting me during this process but every day of my life. Thank you for your wisdom. Thank you for sharing your stories with me and for being so open and willing to share. Thank you for the wonderful example you have set for me and for my children.

To my brother Matthew, thank you for being my partner in crime. Thank you for being my sounding board, and my shoulder to lean on and cry on. Thank you for always being more than a brother but also my friend. Thank you for your honesty and your encouragement. I am blessed and grateful that I had a friend like you to walk this road with. Can you feel that, Matt? It's the heat of the sun. It finally turned its face toward us.

To Maia, what a joy to finally have a sister. Thank you for the love you give my brother and the joy you have brought to our family. I am so grateful for the support you always show me and the love you give to my kids.

To Katie, Amanda, and Lara, thank you so much for your friendship over the years. Thank you for lending me your shoulders and your ears. Thank you for always having my back and walking beside me. You make my life better and me stronger.

To my husband's family, I am so blessed to have gained you as my family. Thank you for your love and support. To my mother-in-law, thank you for showing me love it has been so healing and I appreciate it more that I could ever express.

Thank you to Abby, Linda, and Uncle Paul, for your loving thoughts and words. Your letters blessed us in ways I can't even begin to describe.